BECOME A

CONTENT BRAND

CH
HAVEN

BECOME A CONTENT BRAND

Build a team, own your audience, &

create video your customers will love

VideoFort, INC

DISCLAIMER

The information contained in "Become A Content Brand: Build A Team, Own Your Audience & Create Video Your Customers Will Love" and its several complementary guides is meant to serve as a collection of time-tested and proven strategies that the author of this book has applied to VideoFort INC., his clients and his other companies. Summaries, strategies, tips, and tricks are only recommendations by the author, and reading this book does not guarantee that one's results will exactly mirror his results. Although the author and publisher have made every effort to ensure that the information in this book was correct at press time, the author and publisher do not assume and hereby disclaim any liability to any party for any loss, damage, or disruption caused by errors or omissions, whether such errors or omissions result from negligence, accident, or any other cause. In addition, some names and characteristics have been changed, some events have been compressed, and some dialogue has been recreated. The author will not be held liable for any unintentional errors or omissions that may be found.

The material in "Become a Content Brand" may include information, products, or services by third parties. Third-party materials are comprised of the products and opinions expressed by their owners. As such, the authors of this guide do not assume responsibility or liability for any third-party material or opinions.

The publication of such third-party materials does not constitute the author's guarantee of any information, instruction, opinion, products, or service contained within the third-party material. Use of recommended third-party material does not guarantee that your results will mirror our own. Publication of such third-party material is simply a recommendation and expression of the author's own opinion of that material.

Whether because of the general evolution of the Internet or the unforeseen changes in company policy and editorial submission guidelines, what is stated as fact at the time of this writing may become outdated or simply inapplicable at a later date? This may apply to the resources located at videofort.com/book, as well as the various similar companies we have referenced in this book. Great effort has been exerted to safeguard the accuracy of this writing. Opinions regarding similar website platforms have been formulated because of personal experience, as well as the well-documented experiences of others.

"The media wants overnight successes (so they have someone to tear down). Ignore them. Ignore the early adopter critics that never have enough to play with. Ignore your investors that want proven tactics and predictable instant results. Listen instead to your real customers, to your vision and make something for the long haul. Because that's how long it's going to take, guys."

~Seth Godin, Author, Entrepreneur, Marketer

DEDICATION PAGE

I'd like to dedicate this book to the driving force behind my entrepreneurship journey and my reason for being: my two daughters, Haven and Shea, and my loving wife, Angie.

I'd also like to dedicate this book to the extraordinary visionaries and entrepreneurs I've been blessed to work alongside for the better part of a decade, Steve Gatena and Judy Gatena.

ACKNOWLEDGMENTS

Looking back on the past decade of experiences and knowledge I have obtained and put into this book, it's humbling to know none of this would have been possible without the emotional, physical, and financial support of my family, friends, colleagues, and clients. The very pinnacle of this support, however, came from my life partner, Angie.

A seed was planted in me before I could remember. It took a couple of decades before I finally realized the entrepreneurship drive I possess was derived from my grandparents, father, and mother. Without observing their work ethic, integrity, and hospitality, I'd be a fraction of what I am today.

My hope is that you, too, are inspired by the thoughts and ideas contained in this book to not only create astounding video content, but to build your organization beyond your wildest imagination.

TABLE OF CONTENTS

FOREWORD: HOW TO USE THIS BOOK

The sun had yet to graze the horizon, and my phone chimed loudly enough to wake everyone in the house. But the 4 a.m. alarm wasn't necessary—my eyes had barely closed during the night. My thoughts circled around today's assignment: a commercial for an international energy drink company, flying in the skies above my hometown of San Diego, California.

Yesterday, my concerns were focused on the overcast weather, but looking outside my bedroom window, those worries diminished; I could clearly see the last remaining stars in the sky. I texted my team to make sure they were good to go as the last thing I needed was someone sleeping through their alarm on game day. And as the sun crested, I noticed the weather was even better than I expected—or so I thought.

The coast told a different story. The radio blared in my truck as I hurried down Interstate 5 gazing at a low layer of fog socked in around the harbor and the adjacent San Diego International Airport. Considering the Federal Aviation Agency (FAA) approval needed for a production of this caliber, even a 15 mph wind could cause disruption to our plan. I pulled over to check flight statuses at the airport. Delays across the board. Damn.

The FAA operates much like any government agency, slowly and surely, but with an unparalleled level of detail and stringency. It's what keeps millions of travelers safe every year, and there was no way our production could change that. I texted my team to let them know we might experience delays. Luckily, my inner optimism kept the stress at bay. I continued to our take-off point, Brown Field, steps away from the San Ysidro border and roughly 20 miles from our downtown San Diego jump point.

Our concept was relatively straight forward, in an energy drink sort of way. We were to film my client's skydiving team leaping out of a helicopter toward the downtown skyline in wingsuits, while the stunt pilot barrel-rolled around them in his Zivko Edge 540 aircraft. No big deal, right? The stunt is typically performed by jumping at a minimum of 10,000 feet; however, the only clearance we had received at this point was for 3,000 feet based on nearby airliner traffic. Importantly, all our efforts would culminate in the greater project promoting an upcoming aviation event set to occur at the San Diego Harbor the following month.

The sun was well over the horizon as I arrived at the beat-up hangar where the team prepared. Reports trickled in. Due to delays, our scheduled jumps might be canceled. A staggering amount of work, time, effort, and resources factored into this production. Now it looked like it might end before it ever began because of problems beyond our control.

The day originally promised three jumps: one basic executed by two skydivers (equipped with an American flag, the size of which could cover the entirety of our pilot's plane), and two attempts at the wingsuit barrel roll stunt. Regardless of logistical issues, the entire team remained calm and collected, while I paced in the background, pondering alternative solutions. The time came for our first jump, but the FAA still hadn't called. Our window was so small we decided to get in position just in case approval came at the eleventh hour.

The stunt helicopter took off first, followed by pilot and our aerial production helicopter, mounted with a $250,000 stabilization system and RED Dragon camera. The aircraft flew in formation for the short flight to the landing zone, where they hovered, awaiting a call that would never come. After five minutes, our opportunity closed. We turned back with all the skydivers in tow. The backed-up airport couldn't devote additional resources for our jump. The silver lining? We at least glimpsed an aerial view of the completely clear airport, harbor, and majestic coastline.

Resettling at Brown Field, it became evident that jump approval above 3,000 feet would be very unlikely. To give you some reference, the United States Parachute Association sets minimum pack-opening altitude at 2,000 feet AGL (Above Ground Level) for experienced skydivers, and 2,500 feet for slightly less experienced skydivers. Falling at an average speed of 120 mph equates to approximately 5 seconds of free fall time before divers must pull their chutes. Basically, there wasn't enough time to pull off a barrel roll stunt and barely enough time to deploy a jumbo-sized American flag. We decided to only pursue the flag jump and headed to the Jump Zone to await our second window. Cruising along the San Diego Harbor in our production helicopter, acting like a police escort for the stunt plane, I could hear the roar of the stunt plane's engine through my noise-canceling headphones. Our pilot liked to fly close while in formation. I mean really close. With the tip of his wing pointing toward me, I could've opened the door and hopped onto his plane.

This time, the FAA confirmed our jump from 3,000 feet. Looking at the director's screen, I saw the DP had lined up the opening shot of our divers hanging out of the stunt helicopter. With a quick countdown, the skydiving team jumped from their aircraft and immediately deployed their parachutes, shortly followed by the American flag. No more than 5 seconds later, the pilot zoomed between our helicopter and falling divers, briefly appearing in our camera's sightline. Soon after, the duo touched down in the Landing Zone. We captured 30 seconds of usable footage and at least had something to show for the day.

Returning to Brown Field, everyone involved knew what we shot wasn't good enough to grab anyone's attention, let alone sell tickets for the upcoming event. We still needed the FAA to come through in a big way. Time came for our last jump of the day. Our jumping altitude still hadn't been approved for more than 3,000 feet, but we prepared anyway. If by some miracle, the FAA gave us another 1,000 feet, we could capture something, even if it wasn't what we originally intended. Suddenly, our FAA consigliere brought us good news: "We're cleared for 6,000 feet!" We originally wanted 10,000 feet, but this might lead to a barrel roll or two out of our pilot, if everything went right. And that was a big if.

Four wingsuit divers boarded the stunt helicopter as our camera helicopter took off. To keep up with the skydivers and stunt plane, we had to fly light in the camera helicopter, meaning my linebacker frame remained grounded for the flight. I gave my final thoughts to our Aerial DP, radioed our ground crew on the Landing Zone, took a seat with my editors, then waited, eagerly listening to the radio for jump confirmation.

In the air, we had seven cameras mounted to the stunt plane, another six mounted to the skydivers, a RED camera attached to our chase helicopter, and two ground cameras. In total, sixteen cameras had been deployed for this one jump, and rightly so—this was our last chance to capture something amazing. We didn't want to miss our one chance. As rehearsed dozens of times in their heads, the skydiving team broadcasted a three, two, one countdown, then let go. Within three seconds, the team embraced their formation, hurling toward the South Embarcadero Marina, our landing zone, at over a hundred miles an hour. Meanwhile, our stunt pilot sprang to action.

At this point, there are a couple things you should know. First, the stunt plane was built for aerobatics, not 360-degree vision. Second, he was traveling horizontally, while the divers free-fell vertically, so in order to perform his maneuver at this altitude, he had to fly above them, then dive down to catch up before he could start barreling. This meant the divers were below our pilot's line of sight for several seconds. If he couldn't see them, he had to pull away due to the great risk of a mid-air collision. Literally a second before calling it, the divers popped into our pilot's vision, and he expertly pulled on the handles, throttling the gas and going inverted. Smoke billowed from back of the aircraft, crafting a perfect trail as he hugged the wingsuits' trajectory within a matter of meters. In under 10 seconds, the stunt plane pulled off, the pilots deployed their parachutes, then safely touched down in the landing zone.

The camera helicopter's pilot soon radioed back to our headquarters. "We got it! The jump went great, and we got some amazing footage." Relief flooded my body as we high fived each other at the hangar. Despite last-minute changes and elements outside of our control, we had achieved what we set out to. I must give credit to the entire team for maintaining their cool throughout the entire process. Never did I so much as see one inkling of concern on anyone's face throughout the long day.

This principle is so important for any production. When utilizing a professional and experienced team, they can overcome seemingly insurmountable obstacles, crafting solution-oriented plans based on the available options. And let's be honest, in this line of work, something almost always goes awry. Weather turns on you, people fall ill, actors bail, equipment fails, and best-laid plans change. Murphy's inevitable law will always rear its ugly mug when capturing video content. Sure, you can do everything in your power to prepare for contingencies, planning everything to the second and every budget to the penny, but in the end, it's how you and your team adapt to the unforeseeable that separates the average from the great. The lessons learned from this memorable shoot and hundreds of other projects captured around the world inspired me to write this book.

What you hold in your hand is more than an overview of new media strategies or an introduction to advertising and marketing techniques. It is a handbook to assist you in the choices and creation of video as a branding device for your company or organization. My goal with this book is to offer a clear, easy-to-follow guide that can be used by anyone who is looking to expand brand awareness for their company or their customer's companies. I will begin with a brief history of our modern visual media. Reviewing the past is essential to understanding how we arrived here and imagining where we will go next.

After setting this stage and establishing video's background, I will offer a paradigm shift. Agencies can't alone create the video you need ... yet. Agencies will always have a place in the world, but few can produce the volume and content quality a full-time in-house team can create. Next, TV commercials are dying. They'll work adequately for the next decade or so, with a focus on live events, but the Golden Era for digital is now. This book is intended for marketing professionals and entrepreneurs ages 23 to 55, willing to unlearn "conventional thinking" about video marketing. I want you to understand creating video content isn't daunting. It also isn't expensive, and if done properly, it can be easily manageable.

Here are six core concepts you will receive from reading this book:

- What defines effective video marketing in today's landscape
- Why you should hire your own team: important considerations for in-housing versus outsourcing
- Step-by-step procedures for developing a winning video marketing strategy
- Step-by-step guidelines for establishing an in-house video marketing team
- How to own your audience and stop paying for playing
- How to create a fractionalized video approach for Instagram, Facebook, Snapchat, and LinkedIn.

Before we get into the good stuff, a quick note about the title, Become a Content Brand. In early 2017, I came across a statistic in Adage that baffled me. The title of the article was "Snapchat Video Ads Average Less Than 3 Seconds A View." Three seconds? I'm assuming it's taken you longer to read this paragraph. The basis of the article was that this average view time was leading some advertisers to wonder whether that's enough time to win consumers. User behavior was pegged as the route cause for the brevity. Anyone familiar with Snapchat or Instagram's Stories feature can understand that when you're tapping/swiping through your friends' stories, if something doesn't catch your eye right away, you can quickly transition to the next photo or video. If a forced advertisement disrupts your feed, it's easy enough to tap through to the next post. That is, unless there's something in the ad that catches your eye right away.

What if there was a way to create consistent content that audiences wanted and even searched for? Content that aligned with both the audience and your brand's core values? Content that told a beautiful story and connected a viewer's heart and mind together, leading to a lasting impression versus a quick conversion? I've been privileged to work with some of the world's largest and most innovative brands, creating long- and short-form marketing content for nearly every digital and broadcast channel in existence. Over time, we developed and honed a process that consistently set our production teams up for success, starting from the initial idea creation all the way through post-production. This process is the secret sauce, the magic behind the hundreds of awards we've won on behalf our clients for nearly a decade. And it's this process in the pages to follow that will transform your company into a Content Brand.

It's worth noting that creating outstanding video content is only one piece of your marketing puzzle, albeit a big one. Platforms and audience behaviors change daily in today's digital landscape, and my initial goal for writing this book was to give my readers the tools and processes needed to develop a solid base for their video production efforts for years to come.

CHAPTER ONE: Trial by Fire

In September, 2010, a plan was put into effect to surveil a suspicious compound in Abbottabad, Pakistan. Every movement of personnel inside the structure was tracked. All visitors were documented. Informants were consulted, and even a fake polio vaccination program was used to gather intelligence. The reconnaissance revealed abnormalities indicating someone of significance could be living inside: trash was burned, opposed to being set outside and collected and there was no Internet or phone lines to the upper-class mansion. After several months, the CIA concluded this place was very likely hiding Osama Bin Laden.

The CIA briefed Vice Admiral William H. McRaven, Commander of the Joint Special Operations Command (JSOC), in January, 2011. McRaven worried about the Pakistani response to a commando raid. Additional concerns were raised about the Pakistani government's ability to keep information classified, especially since the compound was located in their backyard. A captain from the US Naval Special Warfare Development Group (DEVGRU) was assigned to work with a CIA team to develop a plan. Initially, bombing seemed to be the easiest course of action.

However, the compound's size and proximity to adjacent buildings meant air raids could result in collateral damage, injuring or killing nearby civilians. Also, it would be difficult to correctly identify Bin Laden if the premises were obliterated. A joint operation with Pakistani forces was briefly considered; however, President Obama decided the Pakistani military could not be trusted to maintain operational security. "There was a real lack of confidence that the Pakistanis could keep this secret for more than a nanosecond," a senior adviser to the President told The New Yorker.

After debating all options, the mission's planners believed one unit could breach the Abbottabad compound without being challenged by the Pakistani military. The Navy's "Sea, Air, and Land" team, also known as SEALs, are one of the greatest special operations forces the world has ever seen. Their main functions include conducting small-unit maritime military operations originating from and returning to a river, ocean, swamp, delta, or coastline.

Trained to operate in all environments, SEALs are elite specialists. *The best of the best.* Each year, the Navy recruits nearly 40,000 sailors for the SEAL training program, but only 1,000 candidates qualify for training. Once recruits enter Basic Underwater Demolition/SEAL school, nearly 75 percent drop out or fail at some point during the grueling 30-month process. The sheer physical and mental capabilities needed to become a SEAL are nearly unfathomable. There's a reason for this level of exceptionality. Once a recruit becomes a SEAL, he is trained to execute precise missions anywhere in the world with perfection.

On April 26**th**, after training in a full-scale version of the compound, the SEAL team left the United States bound for Bagram Air Base. In the late hours of May 1st, approximately two dozen Navy SEALs and a Belgian Malinois (military working dog) boarded modified Black Hawk helicopters designed for stealth missions.

Quietly chopping through the nearly moonless night, the pilots scanned the horizon with night vision goggles. Back in the US, the President and his closest staff breathlessly observed the action in real-time via body mounted cameras.

Prior to the siege, the town's power was cut off. Bin Laden's three-story compound laid dim, its inhabitants unaware of their approaching fate. The first helicopter hovered as the men inside suddenly realized something was wrong. Unusually warm air temperature, combined with the high compound walls, created a vortex ring state, decreasing the Black Hawk's lift and causing the tail to graze a wall. It began to pitch dangerously to its side. Quickly, the pilot buried the aircraft's nose to keep it from tipping over, potentially causing catastrophic damage to the onboard team. Miraculously, everyone survived without serious injury.

Immediately upon crash landing, the SEAL team acted as if nothing had happened. Smoothly exiting the now defunct Black Hawk, they did what they do best: execute missions. Fifteen minutes later, the assault was complete and Osama Bin Laden was dead. Two minutes ahead of schedule, every SEAL boarded the remaining Black Hawk and a reserve Chinook. They loaded up Bin Laden's body, along with dozens of cell phones, electronic equipment, hard drives, documents, and nearly a hundred thumb drives for later analysis.

One of the most widely publicized Navy SEAL missions to date, it sent a message to the world about the capabilities of our elite Special Forces teams. There are many missions the public never hears about, and that is on purpose. From obtaining reconnaissance to capturing a person of interest, SEALs complete their objectives with exacting precision. Largely obscured to the general public, SEALs rarely receive publicized pats on the back. The expert, yet clandestine, unit operates this way because they swore an oath.

In 2010, the world was amazed by the dedication and operational excellence of SEAL Team 6. The fact that SEALS can fly anywhere with sometimes little notice to flawlessly execute orders was inspiring. Now in no way, shape, or form am I comparing what we do at VideoFort to the incredible actions SEAL teams take. Instead, I'm just stating our admiration for their training, processes, and operations. The mastery they display in pulling off the seemingly impossible is something we have strived to develop within our own niche of video content creation. As mentioned, SEALs are often deployed to remote areas with small teams to execute missions while avoiding collateral damage. Taking cues from them, we have tried to emulate their total situational control. It was our goal to be able to travel anywhere in the world within 48 hours to execute a shoot with minimal environmental impact.

When my partners and I first began VideoFort, we didn't understand why the video production industry operated as it did. Dozens of people would arrive on set, yet most of them would stand around for 80 percent of the day. After interviewing union producers and crews, we realized their shoots were even more insane. Not only does every crew member have a specific job, but any of them can be ostracized and even fired for attempting to do something as simple as moving a light or offering a creative idea to someone of a higher rank. (If you're a lowly gaffer or electrician, God forbid you even talk to the Director.)

Intrigued by this phenomenon, we were determined to understand why this arrangement exists. We
sought to find the facts, analyze them, then improve
our own process. We incorporated the fundamental elements, then streamlined everything else. If you have
never been involved with a film or TV production, it
may surprise you how intricately a set is run. If you're
building a new world, like *Star Wars*, or working on
a period piece set in the 1920's, every single production element, from the movement of cameras, lighting,
props and locations, must be meticulously managed.
If not, you'll end up with continuity issues when the
production wraps. The last thing you want is to get to
the editing room and realize a mistake was made at
some point during the process.

In order to control and negate potential issues,
production teams created a hierarchy, not unlike the
Navy, with specific guidelines for communication and
operation. Directors, Directors of Photography (DPs),
1st Assistant Directors, Executive Producers, and Line
Producers typically work in a top-down command
structure. Each position controls the various teams
which report to them. For example, the electricians,
gaffers, and grips report to the DP. Meanwhile, the
actors primarily work with the director. Such delega-
tion establishes a clear line of communication on set.
If you're producing a major motion picture, requiring years to make and millions of dollars to produce,
it's imperative to maintain control and stay efficient
throughout the entire production.

While we quickly understood why this arrangement
exists, this system didn't make much sense for the
quickly emerging new media world. Recognizing every
brand needs online video in some capacity, more peo-

ple on set meant more hard costs for us, thus higher costs for the client, creating an unsustainable model for content creation. Instead of taking the traditional route, we invented our own system. Consisting of nimble three- to 5-person teams, we sourced individuals possessing a variety of skills and abilities: directors who were also great DP's, producers who could not only run a set, but were also great directors, camera operators who were fantastic gaffers, grips who were awesome camera operators. Utilizing these multi-talented individuals was the secret to our success early on and is still a core competency we recommend. You need to surround yourself with such able people to create the quantity and, most important, the quality of content necessary to garner attention in today's digital world.

Around the same time we were honing our operation, new DSLR camera technology launched globally. Vincent Laforet was one of the first filmmakers to create a narrative short using the Canon 5D Mark II. What captured the attention of the filmmaking world was how beautiful Reverie was and, to some extent, still is to this day. With less than $5,000, it was now possible to create digital video that looked like it was shot on a camera system costing ten times that. The DSLR Video revolution quickly became the gold standard of digital video, proving it was economically viable to produce high-quality content without the need of a giant crew or costly production overhead.

If you absorb this book and utilize the resources on videofort.com/book, it is tantamount to video boot camp. After reading the content, you will be able to create a Navy SEAL video department at your organization capable of going anywhere at any time and executing your video objectives with precision. If this task seems overwhelming for your team, at the very least, you'll be able to source and vet an outside production company with these traits. Recent technological camera developments have made it possible to dispense with bloated budgets requiring a substantial amount of people to stand around all day doing nothing. The secrets and tips I will provide you in the following pages will allow you to swoop in like a SEAL (sometimes in the cover of night) to pull off the impossible when it comes to awe-inspiring video content. In order to fully understand how to do this, I want to first review the history of video, especially new media.

CHAPTER TWO: The Mass Media Explosion

"Mass media provides the essential link between the individual and the demands of the technological society."

~Jacques Ellul, Philosopher

VideoFort Makes History

I'm a millennial. Born right smack in the Digital Age, I observed firsthand what was happening media-wise back in high school all the way to present, a period of 15 to 20 years. In my short lifetime, I've witnessed incredible developments in processing speed. It used to take computers more than half an hour to download a 30-second clip. Now, we get furious if our content isn't instantaneously accessible from nearly every inhabited area in the world.

When digital video first arrived, there wasn't one predominant platform and the Internet's bandwidth presented various viewing issues. Storytelling capabilities were limited, mostly relying on stills and animations. When people shared videos, it was accomplished through a variety of ways, often email or via a website. However, with hundreds of video players, everyone struggled to determine how to create content *and* share it efficiently to attract an audience.

Fast forward to 2005 and enter YouTube. Suddenly, there was a central place for housing content. Initially, the quality was what you might expect, considering the majority of households still measured their bandwidth in kbps. It took ages to load a video, until a year later when Google bought the platform, solidifying it as a powerhouse for free content distribution. Around this time, my partners and I formed our first company with the intention of creating digital video content for brands. We saw the opportunity to disrupt how businesses were communicating, not only to key stakeholders, but also directly to consumers. We set our sights on corporate messaging from an innovative marketing and advertising perspective.

My fellow cofounders started our first company in 2009 while attending graduate business school at USC. Back then, I worked at a San Diego-based credit card marketing company. One of the partners had just posted his class project on Facebook: a video marketing a VRBO listing in Santa Monica. Offering a tour of an apartment complex, it was well-shot and beautifully lit with time lapses and even professional graphics (a rarity at the time). As soon as I saw it, I realized that his idea had fantastic potential. Considering he was a former football teammate at the University of California, Davis, I quickly called him to say it was the best real estate video I'd ever seen and asked him to take a trip to meet with me in San Diego.

At the time, he was still playing football at USC and getting his MBA. Broke, he lived in a $400-a-month apartment in South Central Los Angeles with future hall of famer, Clay Matthews. The fact that he could balance school and football on such a high level while launching his first startup intrigued me, to say the least. Not only did I admire his ability to run a company, I foresaw a vision extending far beyond real estate. I didn't know how we were going to get there, but I knew the timing wasn't tomorrow, it wasn't yesterday—*we had to act now.*

We teamed up and began creating content for other businesses beyond real estate, such as hotels and restaurants. Though we didn't have a traditional film background, we saw the possibilities. At the time, YouTube was still mostly playing cat memes, skateboarding clips, and videos of kids pranking each other. With the Internet allowing for free distribution, the opportunities for brands were and still are endless. We decided to create professional YouTube videos for companies wishing to reach their target audience anywhere in the world.

There were hiccups, of course. At first, we didn't know how to run a set, let alone shoot professional quality content. With a little time, however, we eventually met a variety of film graduates that helped us create better and better content. It turned out my partners understood the value of running a good organization. I brought a background in video production and marketing strategy with a focus on narrative: editing, storytelling, and intertwining Hollywood plot devices into corporate videos. Our idea took off, and we went from being a couple of guys working out of a house to opening our first office in 2011.

Initially, people began paying us hundreds of dollars for videos. Those hundreds of dollars turned into thousands, and before long, hundreds of thousands, then millions of dollars. We realized we had a viable company, earning real money. To diversify our revenue streams, we started VideoFort, our stock footage company, in 2013.

When we first began, we knew we needed clients, so we cold-called over a thousand real estate agents, hoping to convince them to pay us to make their video. Most people hung up on us. Others told us to stop calling, but persistence has its benefits. My partner told our largest prospects he was just a starving student trying to change the real estate industry for his Master's thesis. Making sure to email prospects from our USC email accounts, he did everything he could to hack the system, to breakthrough where others have failed. Eventually, he found someone who would listen.

Out of all these phone calls, we connected with Christophe Choo, the great white whale of the luxury real estate market. Christophe understood the unusual nature of the real estate business: highly commoditized on one hand, yet very personal and emotional on the other, with major transactions relying on a high degree of trust and a solid relationship between agent and buyer. Christophe was also cutting edge, embracing all forms of social media, even educating us about Instagram when it first launched.

The reality in real estate is that agents and brokers often work for large, heavily branded franchises, making it hard to create their own individual brand to attract and retain customers. However, the industry dynamics work on an individual level, as well as a franchise level. In any market for real estate (Malibu, South Beach, Manhattan, etc.), there are typically one to three top players who get the lion's share of business. The only way other agents and brokers can compete is by creating a magnetic persona. This personality must be distinctive to others in the market, typically even from the brands they work for.

It turned out Christophe had always wanted to create a *Lifestyles of the Rich and Famous* kind of piece about this swanky area of LA called the Platinum Triangle. Here was this incredible person who always wanted to do a TV series, and us, a couple of untried newbies eager to create a dynamite Internet video.

Our collaboration's first priority was to define what, precisely, would be the "Christophe Choo" brand. Christophe already knew he wanted to be associated with modern, luxurious real estate. He also realized luring customers from established agents in Beverly Hills was not an option. Instead, he would need to focus on an emerging market: millennials, children of his competitor's clients, and foreign buyers seeking to enter the US market.

New media provided the perfect pathway for us. Poring over frequent search terms on Google to discern what people were looking for, we uncovered an engaging title: "World's Most Expensive Homes." This was our big opportunity, thus we put everything into creating the best possible content.

Wasting no time, we appealed to friends and colleagues, begging them to lend us their nicest equipment. We even secured time from the CEO of a prestigious LA-based helicopter company after offering to film the house he was selling for free. Everything seemed to be falling into place, except for one thing. Suddenly, we had a major problem. Several powerful real estate agents threatened to sue us for filming upscale homes owned by their clients without permission.

Fear and anxiety gripped us. We not only had zero resources to fight a lawsuit, we owed thousands in school debt. In spite of the intimidation, and with significant support from our other partners, we put the video up anyway. To put things in perspective, back then, most real estate YouTube videos had low viewership: 50, 100 average views. Ten thousand views meant your video went viral. We released ours, and it quickly shot up to over *two million* views, becoming the most watched real estate video in the world. It remained number one for over three years.

More videos followed, and Christophe became a TV star, won awards, and continued closing millions of dollars in luxury home sales. Our benevolent collaborator became known as *the* luxury real estate agent who understood new media and social media—and as one of the first agents to embrace these tools, his reputation soared. It was an incredible experience for us in many ways, but being able to look back and see how this video helped Christophe is special. Out of all the agents we reached out to, Christophe was the only one to return our calls, cheer us on, and even mentor us as we started our business.

Using the power of video, Christophe stood strong in the face of adversity, differentiating himself from other real estate agents. The result: a distinct personal brand, a reignited real estate career, and high-powered YouTube stardom. Numerous multi-national real estate brands reached out to us after our breakout. From there, we built the leading global real estate production company, parlaying our content creation experience to brands outside of real estate. In our first six of years in business, we went from half a dozen clients to creating commercials and content for over 150 brands around the world, from Fortune 50 companies to multi-national hospitality companies and the largest energy drink manufacturer on the planet.

Throughout my career, two fundamental philosophies have informed my vision. The first comes from Kaizen, a Japanese business ethos extolling the virtues of continuous improvement in working practices and personal efficiency. In general, the idea suggests everything can always be improved. Through consistent practice, this process helped lead my companies and me to extraordinary results. The other influential concept comes from the book, *Zen and the Art of Motorcycle Maintenance.* Author Robert M. Pirsig goes on several journeys throughout the novel, all the time contemplating one key question: "What is quality?" The process of Pirsig's personal discovery reveals the answer is hard to pin down and always in the eyes of the beholder. Pirsig's other insight is that when it comes to solving complex problems, there can be many paths leading to the correct result. In general, there is never one single way to do anything worth doing. The book you're reading may be similarly considered. Though I wish to provide a knowledge foundation, there will be many ways to solve your particular challenges. Ultimately, you must follow your own path, hopefully using these tools and implementing what works best for you.

Both Kaizen and Pirsig's philosophies contain the kinds of nimble, yet deep, thinking required to thrive in the digital age of marketing. If you keep an eye on continual improvement, coupled with an emphasis on delivering quality experiences to audiences, you will succeed in ways unmatched by your competitors. I am not perfect by any means. In fact, I've made many mistakes along the way. Breaking equipment and losing precious footage on hard drives are just a few missteps that come to mind. However, no matter how many times I've floundered, I have tried to learn from my errors and perfect my process. Please use my hard-earned knowledge as a basis for your own journey, and you will be many steps ahead.

It's my intention to provide you the needed steps to be successful in creating and distributing video content for your organization. Considering the myriad new ways small to large businesses now communicate in today's world, the development of an in-house video team or sourcing an outside production company can provide the greatest value for your organization. In the past, companies failed because they couldn't find the right people, develop content relevant or good enough, and/or obtain the viewership to make their efforts worthwhile. However, recent advancements in camera and editing technology have brought us to the point where it is easy to create Hollywood quality content with a small, dedicated team. You just need the right playbook to execute correctly.

Now is the right time for you to put the content of this book in action. The digital landscape has pivoted. Social media channels and audience engagement are constantly evolving and are now more fractionalized than ever. Mobile growth and data bandwidth created an ecosystem where if you don't have an excellent in-house video team or outstanding partners, you're going to be left in the dust. Every organization has the power to entertain their own audience. My mission is to empower organizations like yours to take the reins: to own your content, own your message, and own your audience.

In order to do that, I need to first take you back to where it all began.

Antecedents: Print Marketing's Rise

Advertising may be as old as the human condition, but branded product-based ads did not appear until print advertising became the norm. In Europe, the printing press (invented by Johannes Gutenberg in 1440) churned out journals and weekly newspapers by the 17th century and advertisements became a fixture of Enlightenment-era publications. In 18th century America, Benjamin Franklin was an early adopter of advertising with both his *Philadelphia Gazette* news-paper and later *General Magazine.*

By the early 19th century, Japanese advertisers took advantage of intricate woodblock carvings to print early branding materials just as the medium was simultane-ously developing as a fine art. Also, in the 19th century, European advertisers began expanding into stand-alone print advertising with colorful "trade cards," much like the postcards and fliers still commonly in use today.

Modern print ads, as we know them, owe their suc-cess to the French newspaper *La Presse*, which was the pioneer of paid advertising. *La Presse* used paid ad space beginning in the 1830s to subsidize production of the newspaper, thus allowing it to sell for less and increase circulation for greater profitability. The suc-cess of this single newspaper impacted publications across the globe, forever changing the way most print-ed periodicals did business.

The 1840s was a pivotal decade for branded advertis-ing. The first advertising agency opened its doors in 1841 when V.B. Palmer's Advertising Agency set up shop in Philadelphia. One year later, P.T. Barnum was credited with originating the method of outdoor advertising—the ubiquitous billboards of our modern landscape—when he opened the American Museum in New York City. With seeds firmly planted, it didn't take long before popular slogans, such as Kodak's, "You press the button, we do the rest," from 1888, began to redefine branding.

Radio's Emergence

The first significant non-print content medium com-menced at the dawn of the 20th century as radio ushered in a communications technology revolution. Radio amateurs began conducting experiments with short broadcasts of voice and music signals. In 1908, radio pioneer Charles (Doc) Herrold launched a radio transmitter from his radio school in San Jose, California, and soon broadcasted regularly scheduled programs to local audiences of radio amateurs.

Radio remained a hobby for years, with only a small number of enthusiasts building their own "crystal sets." Once electronics manufacturers realized the potential for experimental radio stations operated by hobbyists, they, too, got into the business, launching their own radio stations. Westinghouse Electric and Manufacturing Company revived 8XK (a 75-watt station) as a fully-licensed commercial radio station in 1920, broadcasting both voice and music programming specifically designed to drive sales of the company's own radio receivers.

After launching four more radio stations in Newark, Springfield, Massachusetts, and Chicago, Westinghouse went on to help found the Radio Corporation of American (RCA), which eventually established the National Broadcasting Company (NBC), a group of 24 radio stations comprising the first United States radio network. In the same year, *The Detroit News* became the first newspaper to invest in its own radio station, WWJ, foreseeing the potential of radio to compete with print media. Other businesses, like retail stores, hotels, and record shops, followed suit, similarly creating their own radio stations.

Not long after, branded entertainment heralded a massive transformation of the advertising industry through content marketing. The early years of radio brought new marketing opportunities, and soap products, such as Palmolive and Gold Dust Soap Powder, took advantage of the opportunity by sponsoring programming as early as 1922, including many serials of the day, leading to the term "soap opera" for these ongoing programs.

By the mid-1920s, the J. Walter Thompson Agency, which handled campaigns for the Lever Brothers' Lux Soap products, had introduced the concept of celebrity endorsements. Their first successful foray into sponsored radio was 1929's *Fleischman's Yeast Hour*, a variety show hosted by Rudy Vallee. It wasn't long before the marketers behind Lux Toilet Soap realized the opportunity to exploit more glamorous material. In 1934, JWT and the Lever Brothers created the *Lux Radio Theatre*, presenting Broadway adaptations and star-studded Hollywood movie adaptations as thinly-veiled promotions of films and, more essentially, long-form commercials for their products.

By 1935, 22 million American homes had radios, and people organized their schedules around their favorite radio programs. Countless images of families gathered around their sets portrayed radio as a central part of American life. By the end of 1939, a radio could be found in nearly 80 percent of American households. This newly ubiquitous medium gave advertisers unprecedented ability to associate their brands with popular entertainment, often through serial installments over the course of long-running shows.

At the same time, the ongoing relationship between radio shows and their sponsors created an unparalleled bond between consumers and brands. Soon, catch-phrases from popular radio shows were penetrating not only the American imagination, but also its idiomatic language with now famous messages like, "We thank our sponsors for making this program possible." Meanwhile, All-American boy Jack Armstrong hocked Wheaties to kids, while the Lucky Strike Dance Orchestra accompanied the American radio (and later television) music program *Your Hit Parade* in a relationship lasting 24 years.

Nowhere is it more apparent how compelling radio content was than in the public reaction to the 1938 broadcast by the Mercury Radio Theater of Orson Welles' *The War of the Worlds*. Based on the popular H.G. Wells novel, and in spite of several announcements during the show that it was, in fact, a theatrical event, the live broadcast was so persuasive it became known as "the panic broadcast." Thousands of listeners reputedly mistook the fictional program for actual news coverage of a Martian invasion.

It's not hard to understand how listening audiences may have been confused, especially listeners tuning in a few minutes late. Cleverly designed "breaking news of events" were coupled with live correspondents pretending to cover an "alien attack." The public responded with genuine fear. Some people fled their homes. Others flooded the police switchboard with panicked phone calls. It was so overwhelming in one small community that a short circuit led to a power outage. If there was ever any doubt radio content could incite people to action, *The War of the Worlds* broadcast vanquished it.

Today, radio may vie with television and the Internet for entertainment and content-sharing, but its roots remain fervently entrenched in our culture. In fact, 93 percent of Americans still listen to radio on a regular basis, with both traditional and satellite services available in cars and homes, even in areas where with limited Internet or local television service. As for Internet users, numerous websites and apps have opened the door for many local radio broadcasters to digitally reach international audiences.

Film and Television Surges

Moving pictures remained mere rapidly displayed photographic stills throughout much of the 19th century. This changed, however, in 1872 when British California governor Leland Stanford hired photographer Eadweard Muybridge to win a bet as to whether all four hooves of a racehorse leave the ground when running. Muybridge became the first to create continuous live action by setting up 24 cameras in a row along a track. As the horse sped along, his camera shutters captured the images frame-by-frame. In 1882, Étienne-Jules Marey furthered this initial discovery, developing the Chronophotograph, the first single camera capable of shooting multiple images. This device took 12 photographs a second, producing a fluid motion effect for the first time.

These two initial experiments soon led to the invention of celluloid film and motion picture cameras. The earliest films were primitive static shots showing an event or action with no editing. Even as storytelling techniques advanced, film remained purely a visual art form until sound became a practical accompaniment in the late 1920s. Unlike radio, whose advertising was paid for by sponsorships, film demanded more from its viewers. Consumers had to leave their homes and open their wallets for the first time. This monetary requirement raised the bar for quality media and audience expectations.

The moving image medium created new and compelling kinds of content: historical narrative, fictional stories, war propaganda, and news. It also allowed for the dissemination of dynamic content in significant and unprecedented ways. During World War I, for instance, armed forces were quick to take advantage of its potential to produce training programs. Meanwhile, a whole industry emerged around generating educational films for schools.

Coca-Cola was the first major company to fully realize the potential benefits of product placement and film marketing. The first on-screen appearance of its brand appeared on a billboard in Times Square in the 1933 movie, *King Kong*. Over the years, Coke ads or actual Coke bottles made appearances in such well known films as *It's a Wonderful Life* (1946), *Bonnie and Clyde* (1967), *Jaws* (1975), and *Taxi Driver* (1976). In 1982, *E.T.* broke the record for product placements with four distinct appearances of the Coca-Cola brand.

This marketing strategy continued throughout the 1990s and into our current millennium, with Coke appearing in award-winning films, like *Million Dollar Baby* (2004). According to anyclip.com, Coca-Cola has far surpassed other companies when it comes to product placement in movie appearances, outpacing its rival, Pepsi. This early adaptor is arguably the biggest and most valuable brand in the world, and it plans to expand its reach even further through a sophisticated content strategy across many platforms, which we will discuss in later chapters.

Continuing with film's placement in the historical context of marketing, it is important to note the appropriation of TV by the film-going public. This development led to content marketing as we know it today. From its inception, television programming encouraged a targeted viewership. For instance, daytime broadcasts of sporting events purposefully fell on weekends in order to motivate male heads of household to buy TV sets.

While television broadcasting began infiltrating the US marketplace starting in 1928, it was not until 1941 that the FCC issued its first commercial broadcasting licenses. Soon, the first television commercial, a 10-second spot for Bulova Watches, aired on NBC's WNBT in New York City during a Brooklyn Dodgers versus Philadelphia Phillies baseball game. Though only about 4,000 televisions were owned in the region at this time, it was undoubtedly worth the whopping $4.00 cost of air time. In spite of its limited viewership, the commercial successfully inspired other companies, American World Airways, Firestone Tires, and the renowned Gimble's Department Store, to quickly follow suit. By 1948, television advertising was so prevalent the American Association of Advertising Agencies formed to regulate commercials.

Brands immediately invested in television, associating their labels with popular entertainment and its stars. TV's first hit show, in fact, *The Texaco Star Theater*, was branded with the oil company name in its actual show title. Texaco employees were featured prominently throughout the hour, appearing as "guardian angels," performing good deeds and singing the opening theme song: 'Oh, we're the men of Texaco/We work from Maine to Mexico/There's nothing like this Texaco of ours! /Our show is very powerful/ We'll wow you with an hour full/Of howls from a shower full of stars.'

Through concerted sponsorship and advertising, the Texaco company rode the television's popularity wave. When Milton Berle (who became known as "Mr. Television") took over the helm, *Texaco Star Theatre* was already credited with driving American television set sales from 500,000 to over 30 million, in less than 8 years.

By the 1960s, psychologists were influencing how advertising also affected the consumer. Many advertising agencies began to increasingly rely on qualitative research, commonly in the form of focus groups. Though their effectiveness is often disputed, focus groups have risen in popularity over the ensuing decades, influencing everything from the financial industry to political campaigns.

More recently, throughout the 1990s and into the 21st century, marketing tactics have proven less predictable, even as budgets have swelled and big brands have tried to differentiate themselves through wilder concepts and celebrity extravaganzas. In 2001, Pepsi produced a $7.5 million ad featuring Britney Spears, opening the door for top tier advertisers to employ the hottest pop icons for their brands. Budweiser's shift from their traditional Clydesdale horses toward the bizarre, but memorable, use of frogs also exemplifies this out-of-the-box thinking, indelibly marking their brand upon viewers' minds.

Just consider *The Tonight Show* as an example of television's extensive reach. Former host Johnny Carson is singlehandedly credited with launching the careers of iconic performers Joan Rivers, David Letterman, Jay Leno, Jerry Seinfeld, Roseanne Barr, and Ellen DeGeneres. TV commercials have always gone hand-in-hand with television. Many commercials became so popular their slogans entered the common vernacular. The single line, "Where's the Beef?" from a Wendy's commercial, became such a popular a catch phrase it was used in the 1984 presidential campaign by Walter Mondale. Another catchphrase, "I've fallen, and I can't get up," still gets thrown around two decades after its first appearance. "Raise your hand if you're Sure," "Trust the Midas touch," and other slogans have proved equally as enduring as the Energizer Bunny itself, which has done exactly as it claimed when it first appeared in the late 1980s: it "keeps going and going and going."

It's clear television and commercials, in particular, have truly impacted our societal landscape and popular culture. Televised jingles and slogans seem to have lives of their own, embedding themselves in the American psyche to such an extent the Super Bowl—annually watched by nearly 100 million viewers—is known as much for its commercials as it is for the game itself.

Nascent Technologies: Internet Television and YouTube

In the 1970s, cable TV and subscription channels expanded national programming's reach through the launch of communication satellites. Hundreds of channels sprang up, from ESPN to HBO, paving the way for 24-hour news networks, like CNN, and niche fare, like the Cooking Channel. So, when the Internet first arrived in the mid-1990s, advertisers were eager to engage the growing network of users.

Agencies saw the potential in reaching millions of consumers, and new media companies sought ways to exploit this burgeoning market. Search engines mined data and created algorithms to connect users to relevant advertisements appearing alongside search results. Ad placement, driven by consumer interest, made advertising part of the conversation. For the first time, consumers were actually choosing the ads they saw based on their own tastes. It was a whole new world.

As connection speeds increased, streaming video prospects finally came within reach. Internet Protocol Television (IPTV), a closed-system of television delivery using data packets, was offered as an alternative to traditional cable or broadcast by the end of the decade. But online streaming services operating in the open Internet were the real game changers, offering free and low-cost content distribution. These new Internet television options included subscriber services, like Netflix, mixed pay-and-free services, like Hulu, and free services, like YouTube.

Streaming media technology allowed users to access content directly from the source, in smaller batches, allowing viewers to consume the data even before completely transmitted. As such, streaming allowed for faster, more agile viewing of online content. Mobile streaming took this even one step further. It no longer even required a computer to receive content. Additionally, the content stayed with the user, whatever the connection, be it smartphone or tablet.

In this post-network era, TV options grew exponentially and content marketing shifted heavily to social media. The Internet provided unparalleled opportunity for content to reach viewers. Unlike traditional television, it made it easy for viewers to access content outside of the home and share the content with other viewers. Suddenly, videos began going viral, sometimes with minimal effort from their creators.

Individuals and brands become household names nearly overnight. On outbrain.com, Will Fleiss wrote in his 2014 essay, *6 Do's and Don'ts of Using Video in Your Content Marketing Plan*, "Video is well on its way to becoming the whiz-kid of content marketing. The form is mobile and dynamic, highly shareable, and, if employed correctly, can be far more engaging than standard text-driven marketing."

Using video as a component of marketing created a social awareness about brands, strategically using content to market content. Companies like Coco-Cola and Toyota weren't just posting effective content on YouTube, they were also embedding this content into their own websites, integrating video images and marketing strategy for a more forceful impact.

With the Internet, Andy Warhol's prediction that in the future everyone will be famous for 15 minutes may be finally close to becoming true. And, of course, some Internet stars have remained famous for considerably longer than 15 minutes. Just take the phenomenon of Justin Bieber. At the age of 12, Bieber posted a video of himself on YouTube. "It had a hundred views, then a thousand views, then ten thousand views, so I just kept posting more videos and more videos," he explained. "Eventually, I got found by my manager who flew me to Atlanta to meet Usher."

It's not just mega-stars like Bieber launching careers without the help of Johnny Carson and other mainstream star-makers. Scores of micro-celebrities, like Sweden's PewDiePie, and the comedy duo Smosh have attracted billions of views and realized profits in the millions through YouTube exposure.

VideoFort Continues Making History

As discussed, in 2013, we launched VideoFort to the public. A stock video company, it's now one of the largest manufacturers and suppliers of HD and Ultra HD (4k) aerial stock footage. To promote our new company, we utilized the kind of content marketing I will discuss in the following chapter. Essentially, our organization created a series of how-to video tutorials and posted them on YouTube for anyone to access. The idea was simple: if we give away free awesome content our target audience needs, we would own our audience.

As you will soon read, VideoFort's burgeoning company's strategy was not so different from the Michelin Brothers' guide for motorists. Wanting to provide valuable content to establish VideoFort as an authority in stock footage, we produced a series of 100 video tutorials to help people create better quality videos, offering information on cameras, editing techniques, and software. We rarely pitched our stock video content, instead we provided valuable information as content marketing that would simultaneously serve to build brand equity.

The result? Within 2 years, VideoFort had over 50,000 subscribers to its YouTube channel and over 3,000,000 views. To put that in context, no other stock footage company possessed anywhere near this type of organic audience engagement in such a short time period. Based on demographics, our subscriber base is primarily comprised of film and video personnel (editors, directors, and creatives), which just happens to be the largest purchaser of stock footage. Capitalizing on just half of those numbers has increased our sales 2,000 percent and our revenue by 20 times. As I learned from building my first production company and working with some of the world's largest brands, content drives traffic, builds brands, and creates sales. This strategy can not only work large organizations, but for any small company, too—and it can most definitely work for yours. In the next chapter, I'll show you how, beginning with an overview of content marketing.

CHAPTER THREE: Content Marketing Changes Everything

"Content marketing is a strategic marketing approach focused on creating and distributing valuable, relevant, and consistent content and to attract and retain a clearly defined audience – and, ultimately, to drive profitable customer action."

~Joe Pulizzi, Founder, Content Marketing Institute

Creative Content Pioneers

In 1900, French brothers André and Édouard Michelin were trying to figure out how to promote their tire business. The automobile was new, and the Michelins understood the best way to sell tires was to encourage more people to take up the hobby of motoring.

They hit on the idea of creating a guidebook for motorists, including maps, car care instructions, and information about local attractions, gas stations, mechanics, restaurants, and lodgings. Presto! *The Michelin Guide* was born. André and Édouard gave away 35,000 free copies of the first edition to their customers. Since then, *The Michelin Guide* has become one of the most powerful and prestigious sources for restaurant and hotel reviews in numerous countries around the world. But it started out simply as an innovative way to sell tires.

What the Michelin brothers believed, and what thousands of business people have learned since then, is that content drives traffic, builds brands, and creates sales. They were early pioneers in the field of content marketing.

Jell-O Offers Value, Not Another Sales Pitch

Historically, advertising has been organized around a direct sales pitch with varying degrees of explicitness and pressure, from a hard sell to a soft sell. But the objective was always singular—to persuade potential customers to buy.

This, however, is changing. Companies still want customers to buy their products, of course, but how they go about promoting their brands is evolving. The future of advertising is all about content marketing: sharing relevant and engaging content, ideas, and entertainment. More important, however, these elements are being skillfully used to establish ongoing relationships between brand and potential consumers.

Content marketing is a central part of what we do as video marketers. Over the course of this book, we hope to demonstrate how it can be instrumental to your approach, too. As a result, we will continually refer to various elements of the strategy throughout the ensuing material. We first described content marketing examples in the previous chapter; now it's time for a more thorough definition.

Content marketing is the dissemination of valuable and consistent information to attract customers and build brands without selling. It is *not* an advertisement to pitch products or services directly to customers. Rather, it is an ongoing process of communication and delivering information meant to empower the consumer, making him or her more intelligent and, ultimately, more loyal.

Although it had been around for years, sales of Jell-O were so abysmal the patent rights changed hands several times in the 19th century before landing with Orator Francis "Frank" Woodward and his

Genesee Pure Food Company in 1897 for $450. Woodward tried a variety of advertising techniques to no avail before considering an offer to sell Jell-O for a mere $35.

However, one of Woodward's investments paid off before ever finalizing any deal. Following the venerable example of *The Michelin Guide*, Woodward tried a somewhat revolutionary technique. He distributed free copies of recipe books and even went one step further by creating a special pan, the now ubiquitous Jell-O mold. Woodward gave this away for free, too.

The idea was simple. The more recipes a consumer wished to try, the more Jell-O boxes he or she would need to buy. The success of this concept turned an underperforming product—one about to be sold for a fraction of its initial purchase price—into a superstar of the parent company with product sales of $1 million by 1906. Fifteen million copies of the Jell-O recipe book later, Woodward renamed his company the Jell-O Company in 1923. Not long after, a merger created General Foods. Between 1934 and 1942, the Jell-O brand took off further, sponsoring the *Jack Benny Radio Show*. Because sponsors controlled radio content at this time, Jack Benny's popularity soon helped make Jell-O a household name. Jell-O also went on to use television tie-ins during the 1950s on through a series of luminaries, including Roy Rogers, Bob Hope, and Red Buttons.

Early Adopters

The kinds of content marketing utilized by Jell-O were consistently rolled out by companies as product tie-ins during this time period. Sponsored programs featured forms of games, decoder rings, and toys associated with products. Advertisers frequently failed on the content side, however, because their messages were too overt.

Still, interesting breakthroughs occurred during the 1930s and 40s in the form of branded entertainment. One such famous success story occurred in 1939, when a Chicago branch manager of Montgomery Ward decided to publish their own children's book as a holiday promotion. Two million copies were given away that year of their original *Rudolph the Red-Nosed Reindeer*, exclusive to Montgomery Ward stores throughout the country.

This was quite a lot of books, especially considering it happened in the midst of The Great Depression. Rudolph quite possibly may have been responsible for maintaining business for Montgomery Ward by encouraging customers to come from far and wide to get their copy, while other retail stores were struggling to bring in traffic through their doors.

In 1986, LEGO Publishing produced nine books and nineteen short films for children distributed throughout Western Europe to promote the venerable company that had been making toys for over fifty years. Around the same time, LEGO also launched a magazine with games, comics, and building tips as part of the LEGO Club. The magazine featured various media franchise tie-ins and occasional educational articles. The idea was the more inspired the consumer became by these LEGO stories, puzzles, and construction ideas, the more building blocks he or she would be enticed to purchase.

The Michelin Guide, Jell-O's recipe books, and LEGO's magazines are all great examples of brands providing valuable information in order to create a network of consumers. These consumers, in turn, are more educated about their products and, therefore, more engaged with those brands. In such a way, the brands have achieved the increased loyalty and improved sales a direct sales pitch often fails to procure. Giving something of value to the consumer proves to be an advantageous sales technique, time and again.

The Internet: Standing on the Shoulders of Giants

In recent years, the scope of business communication has expanded to incorporate many types of new media on Facebook, YouTube, Twitter, Instagram, Snapchat, and LinkedIn. I wouldn't be surprised if by the time you're reading this, another platform has emerged. The strategic use of content marketing provides these brands innovative new ways to connect with customers that simply did not exist in the past. Using skills pioneered by their forebears, these companies possess novel new ways to assert leadership and ownership in their various expertise areas by also providing value, not vapid sales pitches.

"Marketing," according to author and entrepreneur Seth Godin, "Is no longer about the stuff that you make, but about the stories you tell." As content marketing shifts from print material to social media, video is one of marketers' most powerful tools because of its narrative capacity, its immediacy, and its global reach. The story of content marketing, therefore, melds with the story of social media. Nothing in the history of advertising has allowed more people to reach more potential customers than content marketing has through social media applications.

As the 21st century unfolds, the promise of new media continues to grow for content marketing opportunities. However, the general tenets of content marketing remain unchanged: the need to deliver helpful information to empower the consumer. Ideally, this information is also delivered in such a way to encourage the consumer to share with his or her peers. When content goes beyond useful and is also visually appealing, funny, or appropriately "cute," there is very good chance it will be distributed on this very basis alone. In such a way, a company may find its audience spans far wider area than it would have through more traditional marketing and delivery options.

Let's get something straight. Content marketing isn't just about creating a video or telling a good story. Successful content marketing tactics include executions which embody your brand and provide tangible value for your consumers. There are two fundamental questions you should ask yourself and your team before you launch a content marketing strategy.

Is it useful? This isn't just limited to educational content, and entertainment content can be extremely valuable, as we'll learn from Red Bull in later chapters. If your customers benefit greatly from the content and you're confident they'll retain the information presented, then move on to question number two.

Does it pass the logo test? If you were to remove your logo from the end of the video and put a different company's logo into the content, will the campaign still work? Using Jell-O as an example, if you were to switch their product with an apple sauce or whipped cream company, it simply wouldn't work. I'm sure you've watched a commercial before that you completely loved, but seconds after the commercial ends, you have no idea what product or company the commercial was made for. These examples don't pass the logo test, and with content marketing, it's extremely important to integrate your brand into the content authentically in order to maximize your success.

The Grateful Dead: Killing It with Valuable Content

As we've seen, *The Michelin Guide* stands as a clear example of how solid content can be used to raise brand awareness, inspire loyalty, and build a consumer base by offering stand-alone content with an indirect relation to the company's main product. While this particular example eventually spun off into its own success story, it's also instructive to determine how future content may be similarly used.

Giving away value creates a powerful tool for loyalty and continuing sales across all forms of media and with virtually any type of product or brand. The Grateful Dead, by essentially giving away their music to their fans, created one of the most enduring of all touring legacies. To the surprise of music industry executives, it also helped bolster their reputation *and* sell commercial recordings, even as fans readily and openly exchanged their own increasingly professional-sounding live concert recordings.

When the band embarked on their 2015 "farewell" tour, not only were venues packed at every location, the band continued to provide fans opportunities to set up microphones and recording devices in the most optimal locations by the stage. This helpful willingness to give away what many in the music industry consider a band's most valuable asset, the recorded music, may be the Grateful Dead brand's most distinguishing element, allowing the band to be increasingly successful 50 years after their formation.

Not surprisingly, the Grateful Dead were also among the success stories of the Internet revolution occurring between the mid-1990s and the first decade of the 21st century. While online sharing via peer-to-peer networks sparked renewed interest in decades-old recordings of Dead shows, the band worked hard on branding their own online presence. Their site offered the sharing of live recordings, paying homage to the historical privilege of their fans, while also providing a lucrative opportunity for the band to cash in on their commercial recordings, branded merchandise, books, videos, and even special artwork. They understood that if you own the audience, you have more opportunities to interact with your customers, even if that means giving away content that you could have charged for.

The sharing potential of the Internet blossomed during these early years, primarily among music consumers rapidly embracing peer-to-peer networks, like Napster. When the legality of music sharing, and later the sharing of movies via services like BitTorrent, were put to the test, it became clear media entertainment was a primary desire of Internet users and computers were likely the future of media delivery. Content producers, however, were intent on protecting their material, rather than ensuring unfettered access.

Then there was YouTube.

YouTube Changes Everything: PewDiePie and the ALS Ice Bucket Challenge

When YouTube first launched, it was a marginal service for sharing videos produced by novices. By the time Google bought it, however, it was clear these short videos could be lucratively monetized, especially upon going viral.

The concept of the viral video was completely new, original to the Internet, and quite revolutionary in the way media reached consumers. Rather than buying air time or embedding as a paid advertisement, videos were being shared through email, web links, and social networking applications. Sites hosting videos were getting ranked higher in search engines, and as the web evolved, YouTube made it easier to share videos a viewer liked.

Sharing required such little effort anyone could easily do it. Now, suddenly, videos by people with no professional media experience were generating thousands or even millions of hits. Corporations took notice. Many began to buy ad time, but it took a while before the idea to generate their own content really took off.

Among the long list of Internet video success stories, two very different examples stand out. One, the ALS Ice Bucket Challenge, was an awareness campaign designed to encourage charitable donations for medical research. The other, PewDiePie, is one of those phenomena that hits at the right moment and builds upon the social zeitgeist to phenomenal success.

PewDiePie, real name Felix Arvid Ulf Kjellberg, is a Swedish video blogger who became quite wealthy through a series of YouTube videos featuring him playing video games while offering humorous commentary. In the first 5 years of producing short videos for his YouTube channel, PewDiePie amassed a following of over 39 million subscribers and over 10 billion video views. Meanwhile, his channel received over 300 million views per month.

These staggering numbers put him at the top of YouTube's users for several years running and were nothing short of amazing for a college dropout simply doing what he enjoyed, with little idea his efforts would lead to a viable career when he began. Instead, his popularity took off because he tapped, perhaps unwittingly, into an underserved audience of gamers who simply loved his style and personality.

In 2014, PewDiePie started creating content to promote various movies and games through his association with Maker Studios. Using his fan base and YouTube channel, he was able to generate nearly 20 million video views promoting the film *As Above, So Below* from Legendary Pictures. Among other clients, he has also partnered with Mountain Dew on a fanfiction project. Still, his commercial associations continue to steer away from direct endorsements in order to maintain his brand integrity and protect his fan base.

The ALS Ice Bucket Challenge, on the other hand, was conceived as a novel means of raising awareness about Lou Gehrig's Disease. According to *Time*, a golfer in Florida started the challenge. Soon after, various incarnations and similar challenges began occurring. Evidently, the ALS Ice Bucket Challenge struck a collective nerve and became, for a time, an Internet sensation. The basic concept was a person would dump a bucket of ice water on their head and then post the video online, challenging specific individuals to do the same or donate to ALS research within the next 24 hours.

It is doubtful anyone expected the Ice Bucket Challenge to generate as much awareness as it did, or as many donations to support ongoing research into treatment for the disease. This viral campaign not only took off with extraordinary momentum, spurred perhaps by the interactive nature and direct challenging of individuals by their friends and/or associates, it also became part of the increasingly popular genre of "fail" videos showcasing what used to be referred to as "bloopers" or outtakes.

People began compiling Ice Bucket Challenge videos where something went wrong to comic effect, often resulting in an oversized bucket falling on the individual taking the challenge. Several such videos, full of slipping and sliding and plenty of ice, strung together and sent out in an attempt to go viral could create temporary success for a budding YouTube channel practically overnight. The funnier they were, the more awareness ALS received and the more likely it was that the Ice Bucket Challenge would continue. In fact, the charities benefiting from the donations made plans to restart the campaign annually, to take advantage of the summer heat and viral nature of the videos to continue raising awareness and funding for research.

As these two examples prove, there is no doubt sharable content is among the fastest, most effective ways to spread a message. Partnering with the right channel is one way to accomplish this, using a built-in audience with a shared interest. However, beginning with a company's own built-in audience and growing from there is also a highly effective way to utilize this new medium.

In the next chapter, we will further demonstrate the incredible power of the visual medium to capture hearts and minds, while building brands like never before.

CHAPTER FOUR: YouTube, the Video Juggernaut

"You can be a David vs. a Goliath if you get it right."

~Sir Richard Branson

Virgin: Outcool the Competition by Personifying a Brand

In the early 1980s, Virgin Atlantic was a small airline struggling to compete against powerful rivals like British Airways and TWA in a highly-regulated industry. As an upstart business with a plucky attitude, Virgin and its founder/CEO, Richard Branson, knew the brand needed to attract attention to survive. Therefore, Branson embarked on a series of highly publicized stunts to capture the world's attention, including his 1987 Atlantic crossing in a hot air balloon.

While debate continues as to whether or not he actually broke the record for transatlantic balloon crossings, there is no doubt he fired up people's imaginations and curiosity about the Virgin airline. This self-described "adventure capitalist" came to personify his brand. Branson's strategy was smart: outcool the competition to win customer loyalty. He made Virgin an experiential brand and transformed the way people viewed air travel.

Like Jell-O's Orator Francis "Frank" Woodward, Richard Branson is a marketing pioneer who used unconventional strategies to get people excited about Virgin Atlantic. He's since compared some of these marketing tactics to that of being a host at a party. If you're the host and you've invited a bunch of your friends and colleagues who may or may not know each other, you have to be the spark, the connector, to get the fun flowing. If you sit reclused in the corner, chances are, everyone else will stay put. But if you're the first one to jump into the pool, get on the dance floor, or propose a toast, the likelihood that everyone will join in on the fun is substantially greater. You can do the same for your brand. The good news? You don't need to be a billionaire, and you don't need to ride in a balloon. You can use video.

Online Video Audiences Are Growing ... Shocking news, right?

Today's media viewership is rushing to online video, eager to consume digital entertainment. Meanwhile, advertisers are eager to capitalize on this enthusiasm and its potential to cultivate new consumers. The technology company, comScore Inc, measures how users navigate the Internet and offers publicly available white papers with updated analytics.

The comScore data showed that by 2013, 85 percent of web users viewed online video, and video ads accounted for 25 percent of all videos viewed. A report from June, 2014, showed rising mobile use was significant among all adult demographics, with the 18- to 24-year-old group clocking a monthly total of 73.8 hours of use and the 25-34-year-old group slightly edging out that number with 74.6 monthly hours.

YouTube released statistics in 2015 showing a 60 percent increase in hours of watch time year over year, the website's fastest growth in 2 years of already steady expansion. Correspondingly, the number of people viewing video was up 40 percent. These numbers, taken together, show a combination of growing viewership and an increase in the average time users spend actually consuming video. YouTube also reported the average viewing session on mobile platforms exceeded 40 minutes.

In a recent *Forbes* article, Sean Rosensteel explained this web trend toward video is not simply a trend, but is, in fact, founded on basic principles of human biological behavior. He draws upon the work of behavioral psychologist Susan Weinschenk, PhD, who is also a consultant for brands such as Disney, Amazon, and Walmart. On her blog, Susan Weinschenk highlights four fundamental reasons video attracts and holds our attention:

1. **The fusiform facial brain area makes us pay attention to faces.**

   Put simply, our brains are hardwired to look at human faces for meaningful information. Such image processing encourages an emotional connection, which in turn helps us digest information in a deeper way.

2. **Voice conveys rich information.**

   We're programmed to pay attention to the human voice and to interpret that information.

3. **Emotions are contagious.**

   We connect with one another's emotional states, conveyed not just through facial expressions and vocal nuances, but also through body language, which video inherently projects.

4. Movement grabs attention.

We evolved to survive by noticing things in motion. We may not be under the constant fear of being eaten by a lion like our ancestors, but our brains are still designed to pay attention to peripheral movement. In the article, *The Human Brain: Hardwired for Motion,* writer Kris Konrath reminds us that, "movement attracts attention and causes us to pause and assess its relevance to us, while lack of motion does the opposite. Is there any wonder why the motion of digital signage garners 400 percent more eyeballs than traditional signage?"

Visual Information's Incredible Power to Compel

Educators have long understood the power of visual information. A 1996 US Department of Labor publication, entitled *Presenting Effective Presentations with Visual Aids,* concluded 83 percent of human learning occurs visually, with just 11 percent through hearing. This report also notes that the way one initially learns material also affects how that material is remembered.

Drawing upon a 1961 study chronicled in the *Journal of Educational Psychology*, researchers found that after 3 days, subjects retained only 10 percent from oral presentations, 35 percent from strictly visual presentations, and 65 percent from combined audio-visual presentations. That means the combination of visual and oral cues is more than 6 times as effective as the spoken word alone with regard to information retention.

Further academic studies, such as the work of Allan Paivio and Mark Sadoski's *Imagery and Text: Dual Coding Theory of Reading and Writing,* explain the neurological connections that provide for this increased retention. Paivio developed the Dual Coding Theory (DCT) while emeritus professor of psychology at the University of Western Ontario. The DCT explains how distinct channels used for verbal and non-verbal retention can support one another more effectively, because on their own, each channel can only effectively record certain limited details. However, when an image illustrates a spoken point, a stronger internal cognitive connection becomes possible, allowing for greater understanding and recall of more complex information.

The old phrase, "a picture is worth 1,000 words," still rings true metaphorically. It even gave rise to an Internet meme that gained rapid traction when the quote, "A minute of video is worth 1.8 million words" was attributed to a report from Forrester Research. Of course, Forrester Research never published that. After all, if Shakespeare's collected works don't even total a paltry million words, how can one minute of video be worth more than that?

Naturally, it was a joke, cleverly based on the fact that a single minute of video is traditionally 30 frames. So, 30 images every 60 seconds does equal, at least metaphorically, 1.8 million words. While there is no way to quantify how many actual words can be conveyed through an image, what we do know is images are capable of eliciting their own emotional and intellectual responses, enhancing written and verbal input.

Beyond any academic understanding of how sound and image complement one another, we can empirically see this does, in fact, translate to better consumer engagement. On the web, for example, one's chances of getting page-one search results increases 50 times over if a website contains video.

Similarly, on average, a visitor to your site will stay on your page two minutes longer if there is video to watch. Also, more than half of site visitors will watch video before reading any text. The vast majority, close to 90 percent, of online marketers use video, driving 65 percent of viewers to their websites as a result. By 2017's end, video will make up 69 percent of all Internet traffic. To be the most competitive brand possible, video is essential. And of course, video is infectious.

Where Were You When You Saw this Viral Video?

Think for a moment of your own experience with online video. You probably had at least heard of the *Harlem Shake* if you were online in 2013. Throughout 2014, the ALS Ice Bucket Challenge took hold of the collective Internet imagination. Even if you did not participate, chances are strong you know someone who did.

Each of these phenomena encouraged participation through the creation of more videos to be shared with friends and, ultimately, the public. Beyond merely existing as discrete viral videos, they were pop-culture events; some were extremely popular on their own, some furthered the creation of more like-minded content. While stand-alone sensations, like the Gingham Style music video, proved there is no cap on a single video's popularity, the ALS Ice Bucket Challenge showed the true potential for fundraising and, perhaps more important, awareness raising. In the end, however, the lesson is a simple one: online video has an unmatched ability to touch the lives of millions of people.

Save Time and Earn More Money with Video Content

From a practical perspective, online video is one of the best ways to enhance both your business and improve your bottom line. Time is money, and using video in your business will help save you both, while simultaneously driving sales.

Time is a valuable commodity, and video allows for extraordinary economy in any kind of communication, whether internal or external. For instance, using video can dramatically reduce your cost of doing business, beginning with training. All employee training, in sales, operations, and customer service, can be done more cheaply (and probably more effectively) with video.

Video also allows your company to duplicate communications efforts at no extra cost. For instance, imagine you have a workforce of 5,000 people you need to train on a new payroll system. You could delegate the training to local offices and write a long e-mail no one will read—or you could create a training video reaching all of your employees with a consistent message at no extra cost. The other benefit is you can keep using the same video over and over, as long as the content remains fresh. Both the time and cost savings are obvious. Existing human resources can be redirected more efficiently, eliminating potential barriers to training and education.

Video also saves time when it comes to customer service. Housing a video customer service section on your site can allow customers to solve their own problems, avoiding a lengthy call to company representatives. Consider creating engaging FAQ videos your customers can access on their own. The upshot? Customers won't have to wait, and you won't need such a big staff or call centers. Instead, customers can get the information they need easily and efficiently. Everyone's goals are achieved in less time with less effort.

Video also boosts sales by generating higher conversions. Consumers who buy products online feel more comfortable with their purchase decisions if they can see the products in action. Video testimonials from satisfied customers can inform potential new customers and, in the process, help drive sales. In fact, online videos can provide a significantly higher conversion lift. For example, the medical device company, Universal Medical, increased product sales 300 percent by placing product videos on their site to show how the products work and how customers might effectively use them. ComScore studies continue to show consumers who watch videos remain on pages for an average of 2 minutes longer and are 64 percent more likely to make a purchase than other consumers; additionally, professionally-produced video outperforms user-generated content by 30 percent.

Using video can also help you cut costs on staffing and maximize your employees' effectiveness. Repetitive tasks, like on-boarding and other types of training, are easily accelerated through video usage. Video can aid in the sales process: creating a sales video for new prospects covering the basics can help free up salespeople to engage with more potential customers. A 2013 survey by Multichannel Merchant indicated that 71 percent of consumers believe video to be the best way to "bring product features to life." Video created for these purposes ensures everyone receives a uniform experience with a consistently high level of quality.

Further, using digital video saves money on marketing campaigns, while simultaneously delivering better results than more traditional media. A study conducted by Nielsen and the IAB in 2013 confirmed that shifting from television to digital video has the potential to increase your campaign's reach at a significantly lower cost. As Internet use and mobile Internet access, in particular, continue to increase, the value of this extended reach considerably increases.

Influence and Reach: GoldieBlox, Dollar Shave Club, and Lynda.Com

Nothing matches the influence of video, especially for smaller companies trying to make their mark in competition with larger, well-established players. Through video, you can tell your story, be remembered, win new customers, and, ultimately, create brand loyalty.

When video is used to replace humans, it transforms one-to-one communications into a one-to-many model. That can translate to potentially millions. In the past, one-to-many communication depended on expensive advertising or marketing campaigns. Even if you had the money to run ads in national publications or on TV or radio, the shelf life of those ads was prohibitively short; this week's million-dollar print campaign soon became next week's litter-box liner.

The old short shelf life reality is no longer valid with online video. Videos have the potential to live forever. The content may age, but the video itself never expires. Video also works across the boundaries of traditional media, beyond the regional reach of a publication or channel. This allows for continuous discovery and re-discovery. Every month, thousands of new viewers might find your content for the first time. Consider the shelf life of TED Talks or the way viral videos continue to attract audiences long after the initial wave of viewers have seen them. Online video gives you a kind of an unquantifiable storytelling ability, spreading your message through the social sharing of blogs, emails, and instant messages. Your influence is practically limitless.

The personal nature of delivery also enhances the influence of video messaging. When social media or a direct message is used to share content, viewers get to add a layer of personal involvement to the experience. What they are watching now may come from a friend or a source that has been deliberately followed out of a direct interest. Even sponsored media arriving through such means may possess an extra boost of interest because of the association, as well as targeted relevance.

According to the Nielsen and IAB study, switching from television to video in marketing campaigns makes a campaign's reach far more effective, generating an increase in general recall (+15%), brand recall (+33%), message recall (+45%), and likability (+40%). While the potential reach only continues to grow, already the evidence points to the conclusion: online video delivers on its promise. Further evidence is readily available through the many success stories from both established companies and start-ups utilizing online video as their primary mode of messaging.

Consider GoldieBlox, a toy company selling games and books designed to inspire girls to become engineers. Debbie Sterling, the company CEO, trained as an engineer at Stanford, was dismayed at the lack of representation of women in her field. As a start-up in 2013, GoldieBlox created a "stupendously awesome" video illustrating the company's mission. In the video, three little girls sit in front of a TV, watching insipid princess programming. Bored out of their minds, they grab a tool kit, don work clothes, and create a fantastic Rube Goldberg machine that runs through the house and garden, using feather boas, dolls, teapots, kites, and GoldieBlox toys. The inspired video went viral, gaining over six million views in just a few days.

The GoldieBlox video had a terrific impact for the start-up because it staked out a new space in a crowded market and gave the company a foothold against a much larger competitor, Mattel. What's more, it activated people's imaginations. It prompted a national discussion about the role of women in science and engineering. It turned something arcane, toy design, into something fun, engaging, and socially conscious. And all of this with the company name at the center of the discussion. Great stories told on video can make a significant impact and are remembered far beyond any single moment of fame.

The Dollar Shave Club had a similarly audacious idea: to go head-to-head with Gillette, a powerful company owned by the global powerhouse, Procter and Gamble. To carve out a niche in the disposable razor blade market, The Dollar Shave Club had to upend marketplace expectations.

Dollar Shave Club's CEO, Michael Dubin, is an alumnus of the comedy troupe, Upright Citizens Brigade. He brought his comic skills to the table with an online video featuring a shaving baby, a guy in a bear suit, and Dubin himself, swinging a machete. With the eye-catching title, *Our Blades Are F**king Great*, Dollar Shave Club's video crashed the company's server in the first 48 hours, followed by nearly 5 million views on YouTube in the company's first 3 months. In 3-1/2 years, by October 2015, it had nearly 21 million views on its official YouTube page alone. Other YouTube channels reloading the video showed ranges from 10k to 40k additional views of their own, making it difficult to gauge the full, extraordinary range of this video's success or reach.

Dubin understood how video makes for memorable experiences. "When you're launching a new business, and sharing a new idea, if you can get people to remember it, there's obviously a better chance at success. I have always believed in the power of videos to tell stories," he was quoted in the September 2012 issue of *Entrepreneur Magazine.*

The results were immediate. In the first 48 hours after the video appeared on YouTube, 12,000 customers signed up. Even more impressive is the fact this video, in conjunction with just a few Google ads, is the only marketing The Dollar Shave Club pursued to launch their brand.

The training website Lynda.com is another excellent representation of video's powerful reach. Beginning as a software training company, Lynda.com now offers thousands of educational videos, with topics ranging from K-12 education, to photography, and project management.

Lynda.com's training videos are watched by viewers around the world. The global impact can be seen with students in the Philippines and Kenya learning how to use Adobe Creative Suite and becoming graphic designers, allowing them to compete for work with graphic designers in England and the U.S. via sites like UpWork.com and fiverr.com. Through online video training, people in developing countries are now learning skills previously restricted to the developed world.

Individuals can join the new global workforce, not as factory workers, but as skilled employees, literally because of video.

Ultimately, the takeaway is it does not matter what kind of business you are in—video can help you tell a story to attract and engage viewers. In addition to these examples, disparate organizations, from animal charities to oil companies, have begun using video to harness the "movie magic" of Hollywood, creating compelling stories with emotional impact that makes for the most memorable message.

CHAPTER FIVE: What is an Innovative Video Marketing Strategy in Today's Changing Business Landscape?

"No matter what you do, your job is to tell your story."

~Gary Vaynerchuk

A Glimpse of the Current Evolving Landscape

There is a real lack of content out there on how to develop your own internal video marketing team. Consequently, I want to give you tricks and methods to not only build your own in-house group, but also shape your own people to perform at ad agency level. Not only that, I want to offer you indispensable content strategies for the big five Social Media Platforms: Facebook, Instagram, YouTube, Snapchat, and LinkedIn. However, be advised the content you create can *and* should be distributed anywhere and everywhere your audience's attention resides. My approach is a soup to nuts solution: how to go from zero videos to an internal team annually pumping out hundreds of quality content pieces. It is also my intention to help you more fully understand marketing strategy, content development, production, and distribution.

Video marketing has grown in primarily digital ways. It has evolved from being an entity once known as film, something so grainy and fuzzy you couldn't always make out the picture. Earlier sound quality wasn't much better. It often required concerted listening to put the pieces together. The incomparable quality of videos today can be so striking it can feel like you're actually in the room with someone, fully experiencing what you are witnessing. However, far too often, I see brands mismanaging content and producing dreck comparable to what my toddler shoots on my iPhone. You must be willing to take the time to at least match the quality of your competitors; audiences are far too accustomed to this high caliber to appreciate anything less.

Digital content, or 2D content, as it exists now, will only continue to improve in quality. It's the stories within the videos themselves that will separate successful campaigns from failures. This storytelling aspect is what our team works on bettering every single day, and it should be a key element in your process. When we first started our company, we had the opportunity to work with brands whose content was adequate at best. Yes, they were creating "video," but the quality misrepresented and undermined their brand. We developed a new approach to their digital video content, acting as storytellers from a corporate communications standpoint. Our goal was simple, to generate as much viewership and engagement as possible.

From a philosophical standpoint, deep questions hover over the implications of video technology as it evolves by leaps and bounds. *Are we witnessing the seeds of The Matrix or some similar dystopian future in which people succumb to virtual reality addiction because it's better than real life?*

VR is, for lack of a better terminology, simply a complex delivery of immersive digital video content, whether it be live-action or animation. The user experience is also continuing to evolve; in our lifetimes, we will no doubt witness the shift from passive viewership to active viewership; from a person watching a story to a person *participating* in a story.

It's becoming clearer and clearer we are living in the final moments before the widespread adoption of virtual reality. It's been so gradual most people haven't given much thought to what this shall mean. Similar to the Internet's upending cultural paradigm shift, VR will completely alter how we consume media. Think of it this way: in 1995, you could easily count the number of websites in existence. Due to bandwidth constraints, web pages consisted of simple text and small images. Few had access to the Internet, and even fewer had PC's capable of displaying sophisticated website information. Yet, only a couple decades later, high-speed web access has become critical to our everyday existence.

As of this writing, virtual reality is a novel entertainment platform; however, this trend is bound to change in ways as dramatic as Internet adoption. A 2017 study conducted by eMarketer predicted 9.6 million consumers will use a VR headset at least once a month in 2017. By 2019, that number will reach 17.2 million people, or 5.2 percent of the U.S. population. Though virtual reality has been slower to catch on in the US, don't expect mass adoption until a corporation brings it to the masses. My prediction is we'll continue to have lackluster user adoption until Apple launches a VR platform or headset. Currently, 40 percent of US smartphone users own an iPhone. Given the fact that iPhone boasts one of the best screen resolutions in the marketplace, I can only assume VR will be more widely adopted when Apple throws a headset into the ring. When we evolve from passively watching screens to actively engaging in what we see, video marketing will change, too, allowing us to participate in the experience. It's important to qualify this prediction by way of analogy, however. Active viewing won't replace passive viewing. Just as iTunes didn't displace the radio, both will simultaneously exist as they offer different things.

Social Media Players and their Effect on Digital Marketing

You can think of social media platforms as channels. Twitter is just a channel, just like TNT is a channel. Many channels come and go; and while it pays to be an early adapter of a new channel, it's more important to create content where a critical mass can find it.

Anytime a platform dies, we can typically derive the root cause as an audience shifting to a new or separate platform. There will always be reshuffling. Like the live users interfacing with it, the Internet is dynamic. The world of social media fluxes with audiences dipping in and out, posting content, responding, and reacting. Popular spots attracting traffic through unique storytelling is where digital video will continue to live.

On the other hand, the same fractionalization trends of TV will most likely impact the web. Once upon a time, there only three TV channels. Now there are thousands. It's conceivable to predict infinite growth amongst different platforms offering video. What matters more than the players involved, though, are the actual ongoing strategies behind the channels.

For instance, a seemingly broad horizontal channel like Facebook obviously contains more than just your news feed. It has sub-channels to cover many other content categories. If you want to visit the National Geographic Facebook channel, you go to the Facebook page for that content. It's horizontal, and thus has many content categories. Facebook is also unique because it's acting as a hybrid of on-demand programming and traditional linear programing. You can get National Geographic content whenever you want (on demand), but there is also a live stream that happens at a scheduled time (linear programming).

The emerging platforms purposefully begin broad. A channel-like platform (Facebook) will cover a small amount of content over a wide number of categories (news, travel, business, sports, etc.), becoming horizontal. Craigslist is another example of a horizontal platform because it is a broad-spectrum listing service. It includes multiple categories and has proven ideal for selling a car or renting your house.

Eventually, all of the horizontal platforms become "verticalized" or unbundled. For example, ESPN became the sports-only channel. It removed all sports news and programming from channels, like CBS, NBC, ABC, and FOX. If someone wanted to consume only sports content, they would simply turn on ESPN. Similarly, Internet companies are now being unbundled. With Craigslist, for example, there are niche platforms specializing in just one of Craigslist's offerings, such as Airbnb for renting homes or Cars.com for selling cars.

Even major players, like YouTube and Facebook, have come under attack by companies like Twitch.com and Pray.com. Twitch.com, now owned by Amazon, is a hybrid video streaming platform and social media platform specializing in e-sports (videogame) content. Pray.com is another new media company specializing in faith-based content and faith communities. For a broad platform providing on-demand content, discoverability remains the primary challenge.

The smartest brands know how to overcome this hurdle by leaping into established platforms with critical mass and attention, an advantage offering significant momentum. When properly done, this is a great way to take advantage of low advertising costs. Those first big brands into Facebook received the exclusivity of eyeballs for pennies on the dollar. Anyone else leveraging emerging platforms as early adopters are in a similar boat. Early adopters hit a window usually lasting somewhere from six to eighteen months. This is the best time to get your content in front of audiences at the lowest cost.

Pura Vida Bracelets exemplifies this phenomenon. I've had the privilege of knowing the two founders, Griffin Thall and Paul Goodman, for over a decade. After graduating from San Diego State University, Paul and Griff took a trip to Costa Rica, unaware the trip would forever change their lives.

Sometime after one of their numerous surfing sessions, they crossed paths with two bracelet artisans named Jorge and Joaquin. Their colorful handmade bracelets seemed to capture the essence of the creators' journeys. At the time, Jorge and Joaquin lived in poverty. They slept with their family in a single, crammed room with three beds and sold bracelets in order to stay alive. After seeing this, Griffin and Paul asked Jorge and Joaquin to make 500 bracelets to take home with them. The Ticos (Costa Ricans) looked at Paul and Griff dumfounded. They only had maybe a hundred bracelets on them, and would need to buy more string to make extra. At the time, Paul and Griff didn't know their plans with the bracelets; they simply wanted to help these two out, bring some souvenirs back home, and maybe make a couple of bucks in the process.

Jorge and Joaquin set to work. With Paul and Griff flying out of Costa Rica the next day, the bracelet-makers couldn't spare a single moment. And this was a big deal for them. Fulfilling this order meant eating well for the next month, instead of barely scraping by. Accordingly, they spent the entire night tying, braiding, and stacking what would be the first unofficial order of Pura Vida Bracelets. The next morning, Paul and Griff met up with the visibly exhausted Ticos and were amazed they delivered on their promise.

Paul started thinking about the numbers. "If we take these 500 bracelets back to the US that we bought for $.50, and sell them for $5 apiece, we would pay for our entire trip." Paul and Griff started to get excited as the numbers and scale grew in their head. "If we sell a million bracelets, that's over $5 million!" In theory, this was correct, but they didn't have a plan for *how* to tell sell bracelets to hundreds, thousands, or millions of individuals. One other small problem emerged through the excitement. Jorge and Joaquin didn't have cell phones or computers.

Paul and Griff, therefore, took the Ticos to an Internet café down the street. Paying the $10 fee to access the web, Paul gave Jorge and Joaquin a quick rundown of Gmail. Very quick. Their airplane would take off soon, and even if tropical rainstorms didn't delay traffic, they needed a good couple of hours to get there.

"Okay, we're going to go back home and sell these," Paul said. "I'm going to send you an email in a week and let you know how we did, and how many more bracelets we need." Mind you, Paul and Griff spoke about as much Spanish as Jorge and Joaquin spoke English. Jorge looked at Griff, picking up every other word, watching his every move. Joaquin chimed in, in Spanish, whenever he recognized a word. After the crash course, they set a plan. Paul and Griff would head home, bracelets in hand, and the Ticos would check their email daily. No one would have expected this casual encounter to grow into what it is today.

Paul and Griff threw the bracelets in a bowl at their house and started selling them to friends and family, eventually striking up a conversation with a local boutique shop who said they could probably sell the bracelets for $5 to $10 a pop. Before long, their bowl of bracelets was empty. Paul emailed Jorge and Joaquin. A couple of hours went by with no response. Paul got worried. Here they were making progress on their first tipping point, and their supplier wasn't responding. Suddenly, Paul looked up to see an unread message in his inbox. "Hola Paul. ¿Cuantós quieres?"

Paul placed an order of 5,000 bracelets. I can only imagine the face of Jorge and Joaquin when they saw this email.

Pause. I'd just like to recap the story for a second. Two 21 year olds travelled to a third-world country, met some nearly homeless locals, bought some string bracelets off them, went back home, made over $1,000 off of the bracelets, and now were about to send hundreds of dollars to a couple of Ticos with no guarantee they would ship the next set of inventory. Still with me? Good.

Luckily, Jorge and Joaquin once again delivered on their promise, and the bracelets arrived in beautiful San Diego. Paul and Griff had no real desire to go door to door selling bracelets. The boutique route was interesting, but not scalable. Selling the bracelets online and directly to the consumer made the most sense, so they quickly asked the question, "How do we get customers to our website?" In answering this question, they found a short code on Facebook where they could invite every one of their friends to like a page. The "hack" has since been patched, but this is an example of taking advantage of a platform early.

The business partners began going to the library every night, giving out free bracelets to anyone who would share Pura Vida Bracelet's Facebook page with their friends. One hundred followers turned into 1,000, 10,000, 100,000, and now over 1.3MM followers on Facebook alone. They are now the number two most engaged jewelry brand on Instagram with nearly 1MM followers, beating out the likes of Tiffany & Co, Hublot Geneve, Rolex, Cartier, Swarovski, Pandora and Bulgari—to name a few. Of course, their success hasn't been hinged solely through viral fellowship, but that is how they started their momentum. Once someone ventured into their ecosystem, the content kept them there, converting them into Pura Vida Bracelet enthusiasts.

This is an innovative way to capture a large audience, but in a very rudimentary sense. You could only accomplish something like what Pura Vida Bracelets pulled off at the time with Facebook because it was such a new platform in the process of emerging. Since the product was targeted to college students, it was the perfect method for launching their fashion/jewelry company.

Fast forward to today. Pura Vida Bracelets is now a multi-million company creating video and social campaigns with a robust following. More important, through their give-back campaigns, they've donated over $1.5MM to various charitable organizations since their company's inception. With the breadth of their fanbase, they can communicate with their fans and potential customers without having to pay for advertising.

They're also primarily a digital company utilizing various social media platforms. They employ the newest channel to do what they do best: sell cool bracelets, and now apparel, and engage their target audience, inviting them into their ecosystem where they own everything from product creation to distribution. What amazes me about their success to this day is the fact that they didn't launch a new technology. Their products don't solve a big problem, and there were thousands, if not millions, of bracelet products in the marketplace already. Despite all of these potential roadblocks, they succeeded beyond expectation because they were able to capture their audience's attention.

This is just one example demonstrating how to take advantage of fractionalized platforms. It doesn't matter if it's Instagram, Snapchat, Facebook, or Twitter. Pura Vida Bracelets constantly triumphs, gaining audience attention because they know who their target is and how to offer them value through owned and earned media. They are the real winners of social media, utilizing the lowest acquisition costs to gain long-term customer loyalty by leveraging platforms and creating innovative content.

Now that we have observed a success story of a brand leveraging social media to grow and monetize their audience, let's explore the big five social media channels in depth. Understanding the content applicable to each of these platforms will give your marketing team the greatest probability of success in the months and years to come.

Characteristics of Successful Content for Every Platform

Story and strategy are paramount to any video marketing plan. Simply creating a video for its own sake will most likely (99.9 percent of the time) not bring you the results you seek. Employing a thoughtful strategy while delivering a compelling narrative to promote your brand continues to be the only tried-and-true method for successful video marketing.

When it comes to content, education is scalable. As touched on in the previous chapter, any time you can educate somebody through a video—whether it be on-the-job training for a new employee, teaching a customer how to use your product, or bringing deeper awareness to your service—the rewards are manifold.

The power of video to reach hearts and minds is priceless. As we touched on, using video can save you hundreds, if not thousands or millions, of hours. Regardless of the platform, the benefit is the same: the ability to distribute ideas, information, and thoughts to mass audiences. No matter the venture, education scale, or challenges surrounding your business, video marketing will pay dividends every single time, guaranteed.

Now that we understand content is king and which content is applicable to each respective social media channel, let's discuss pros and cons of in-housing versus outsourcing when it comes to creating your brand's videos.

Facebook

While Facebook users span the widest range of consumer demographics, the site's algorithms are most advantageous for news sources. Still, with this knowledge in hand, and a sharp focus on engagement, all business can utilize Facebook to grow their brand and increase their organic reach.

In January 2018, Facebook once again changed its algorithm. By doing so, founder and CEO Mark

Zuckerberg hoped to "prioritize posts that spark conversations and meaningful interactions between people." To host these opportunities for conversation, Zuckerberg's new format gives preferred visibility to credible news sources. This shift will favor positive, educational content over promotional ones. Within this realm of beneficial content, the algorithms favor live videos—on average, user interactions increase six times with this content as opposed to pre-recorded video. In total, live and pre-recorded videos will remain at the top of the most visible content.

So, how do you specifically use video content to take advantage of Facebook's algorithms? A brand engaging with their Facebook customers should post content for the purpose of getting reactions, specifically through comments. The video will have greater impact if users in the same friend or family groups comment to each other on the post. Translated, this means you should pack as much info as you can within the first few seconds of a video post, either with eye-catching headlines or shocking visuals. Other posts should capitalize on current events and current news headlines. The greater relevance in these posts, the more likely users are to share their opinions, comment and engage in discussion, and thus heighten the virality of your content. There are several keys to creating content for Facebook's audience. Your content must be relevant to a specific audience, even going so far as creating variations of the same content for different demographics. If you're Walmart for example, a 65-year-old male is going to engage with vastly different content than a 23-year-old female. And if your goal is to drive more traffic to Walmart.com, each demographic should fea-

ture products relevant to said group of people. Long
dead are the days of advertising a $99 TV to everyone.

Tactically, your content must work both for mobile
and desktop and with/without video. Closed caption-
ing has come a long way on Facebook, but it's important that you think through how someone is going to
watch your ad and make sure you're in the clear for
every instance—on their phone while commuting to
work on the train, in their office without headphones
on, between commercials during a sporting event ...
etc. At VideoFort, we noticed a 15 percent increase
in viewership on our content simply by exporting our
videos in a square 1:1 format vs the traditional 16:9
widescreen. We attributed this increase was due to our
content lasting on a user's screen for a longer period
of time, allowing them to watch more of the content
between scrolling through to the next post.

LinkedIn

LinkedIn is an online job market most used by millennials, aged 18 to 29. It captures the attention of many
post-grads looking for work, as well as business owners seeking to expand their reach. Seventy-five percent
of LinkedIn users possess incomes over $50,000, and
50 percent of B2B buyers use LinkedIn when making
purchasing decisions. With a news feed similar to social media, and another platform prioritizing video over
written content, LinkedIn is a prime outlet for marketers and companies with high-end video production.

LinkedIn's algorithm prioritizes native videos, or
videos hosted only on the site itself (rather than a
hyperlink or embedded YouTube video). When scrolling, these videos play automatically, and a user only
needs to watch it for three seconds to count as a view.

However, because LinkedIn users often swap links and articles, we recommend companies use a mixture of both text-only content and eye-catching videos. Specifically, these videos should contain information you wouldn't be able to find in a related article. It's key to track text versus video engagement to understand which your business should prioritize. Either way, housing a few videos on LinkedIn will help visually represent your brand, showcase its products and services, and distinguish it from other companies.

It's important to understand that the user behavior on LinkedIn functions much differently than Facebook. Whereas Facebook users are more likely to scroll their timeline to kill time, connect with friends and family, or review and absorb news and messaging, LinkedIn users are more likely to engage with content on the platform to grow professionally. According to a survey conducted by LinkedIn in June of 2017, 62 percent of LinkedIn members said the reason why they engage with content on the platform is due to the content's educational or informative nature. The top 3 topics that drive the highest engagement include Industry Trends/News, Tips & Best Practices, Jobs & Skills. For a link to the full article, go to videofort.com/book.

What this means for video marketers is that entertainment content is less likely to be engaged with on LinkedIn versus educational and industry trends related topics.

Twitter

Most users, aged 18 to 29, use Twitter on their mobile devices, and 82 percent of them watch videos on this social media platform. With the newly revamped 280-character posts (up from 140) and the booming presence of hashtags, Twitter makes it easy for businesses to grow a faithful following. Since content is so short, users are more likely to share what they see, and Twitter flourishes as a discovery tool, instead of a search engine.

Additionally, Twitter recently updated its reverse-chronological system to an algorithm-based feed which, similar to Facebook, will focus on content with comment/like engagement. Since these algorithms can be turned off in settings for savvier users, it's important you create high-quality video content to ensure your content is always incredibly watchable. Since Twitter posts are naturally more eye-catching than lengthy Facebook posts, businesses should tease longer content hosted on a business's website by using short clips over a set period of time. This will boost social media engagement and website traffic and continue to increase the number of followers.

However, from a video perspective, and in my humble opinion, I wouldn't focus on gaining your Twitter following as a tactic to grow your business. It's a great platform, which rightly has its place in the social media world; however, we frequently advise clients to use their Twitter following to drive traffic directly to their website, where their video content resides.

Instagram

Instagram, the most image-centric platform out of all the social media channels, attracts a similar demographic of adults aged 18 to 29 (59 percent of users). The app also prioritizes video, creating real-time engagement opportunities to ensure posts will appear at the tops of newsfeeds, and utilizes "autoplay," so users don't even have to click on the video to watch.

Furthermore, once Instagram realized users missed about 70 percent of their news feed, they switched from a chronological feed to an algorithm that tracks users' interests. This attempts to prioritize content in the same vein to share to users' news feeds.

To ensure your posts sit at the top, use the recently developed Instagram Stories as engagement opportunities: post videos likely to be replayed by your audience or that are shareable among family and friends. Since Instagram prioritizes live streams even more highly, aim to shoot live at least once a week. Users are notified whenever you're shooting live, allowing them to interact with you in real-time. Utilizing live-stream, along with HD photos and relevant hashtags, will ensure your content stays relevant to the site's algorithm.

From an advertising perspective, many of the tactics aforementioned in the Facebook section hold true for Instagram. Additionally, your stories should be consistent, relevant, and entertaining with a focus on video versus images alone. Integrating stickers, GIFs, texts, hashtags, and polls are all great ways to increase engagement and keep users from swiping to the next story.

Snapchat

With 300 million monthly active users (71 percent under the age of 34), Snapchat dominates the image and video-based platforms for social interaction. Snapchat only shows pre-recorded and paid advertisements alongside users you already follow.

Snapchat's limited capabilities offer tradeoffs. It's difficult to discover new users; however, with a pre-existing follower base, engagement rate boasts 4 times higher than Instagram. A brand posting "Snaps" on the app can achieve the same reach with 100,000 followers as it would with 2 million on Instagram. Posting is also more economical: unless you're creating a professional advertisement, Snapchat users don't expect high production value. Instead, they want to feel personally involved with your brand through the quick and efficient interface, lightening the workload.

Similar to Instagram Live, business owners should take advantage of Snapchat videos for real-time engagement. These can include Q&As, current events, or a behind-the-scenes look at your company. Users can reply with individual snaps and participate in polls, Q&A, direct feedback, and questions. This unique type of engagement harbors dedicated, loyal, and curious followers. You can also include a discount or promo code in your Snaps with a "swipe-up" link to increase conversion rates. And make sure to include a link to the company's site for cross-platform CTR. Revealing the inner workings of your company through video affirms your trustworthy nature and can further increase brand loyalty and customer retention.

CHAPTER SIX: Should You Hire Your Own Team? In-Housing Vs. Outsourcing

"If you hire people just because they can do a job, they'll work for your money. But if you hire people who believe what you believe, they'll work for you with blood, sweat and tears."

~Simon Sinek, Author

What is an In-House Team?

An in-house team is a group of people fully capable of producing, shooting, and editing video content, particularly digital, but also broadcast media. Teams typically consist of a "Preditor," one person responsible for fulfilling all of the video production tasks.

Preditors are usually only suitable for small businesses. A more sophisticated crew beyond the bare bones minimum can range from a two-to-three-person production unit with a director, producer, an editor, to a high-budget outfit utilizing a dedicated cinematographer and audio technician. Below is a more detailed description of the various roles and responsibilities.

The Director: Primarily responsible for overseeing the video's assembly. Working at the center of video production, this person transmits the vision to audiences through the cinematic medium. He or she will most likely create or refine the idea, develop the script, work with the talent, interface with the production team, and possibly shoot the content to bring the story to life.

The Producer: The project manager tasked with establishing and implementing an organizational plan for production. This group leader handles the scheduling and manages every aspect of production, from start to finish. Producers are generally problem solvers, continually finding ways to fit all the different puzzle pieces together, while ensuring everyone remains safe, fed, on time and on budget.

The Editor: The creative individual who shapes the raw footage into a cohesive story through the use of editing software to manipulate various pieces of content. This person may also engage in more complex post-production activities, such as obtaining music to aid the material, as well as collaborate with voiceover artists to augment the finished product. Typically, the best editors focus on editing, not performing double-duty as director; however they can also hold on set positions, such as a Digital Imaging Technician, who is responsible for image quality control, on-set color correction, and managing a production's workflow.

Cinematographer: Also known as a Director of Photography or DP, this person captures the action on film or video. Though more cost-conscious budgets may rely on a director for shooting to reduce costs, utilizing a dedicated cinematographer can elevate the production, especially when it comes to lighting and other technical capabilities.

Sound Technician: The on-set audio expert. Be warned. The biggest mistake in-house teams make is not assigning someone to strictly handle audio. The difference between an amateur and a professional video is typically sound quality. Too often overlooked, sound is an integral part of releasing a quality product. Bad sound can undermine an entire project. Please note:

a dedicated in-house person isn't necessary. Individuals may be hired on an as-needed basis but should always be a part of every production. One more quick tip: when capturing dialogue, be sure to always mic people separately because many of the very best cameras still don't capture great audio.

The Preditor Approach

It's possible to find solid people skilled in each of the above departments; if your budget allows, you can segment the various roles, giving niche duties to each person to fulfill their role. However, what can be especially helpful for a small business creating content on a shoestring is to employ the Preditor approach. Not only is the Preditor a jack of all trades, meaning he or she can shoot the video and edit it, this person is a master at bringing together the overall vision from all the moving, disparate parts. Go to videofort.com/book for more information about building your team, including average costs, hiring practices, and tips to hire your ideal production staff.

A Filmmaker Versus a Video Marketer

We have worked with many film school graduates. For the most part, they understand effective storytelling but don't always know how to sell products or services. Here's a story to illustrate what we mean.

We were creating an online video for a multi-national luxury real estate brand, emphasizing the mythology behind their company's origins. The crux of the video was that the founder was one of the first people to wisely utilize video way back in the 1920s to sell real estate. Similar to what we would one day create with *The World's Most Expensive Homes*, our client's company once used some of the very first planes and cameras to film luxury properties, which they later showed to buyers all over the world.

For our video, we created a nostalgic period piece celebrating what the innovative company once pioneered nearly 100 years ago. We transitioned from old-school, black and white images, to a modern-day aesthetic demonstrating how the company operates today. The post-production process was insane. Since the client wanted to showcase the project at their upcoming, national conference (located thousands of miles away in New Orleans), we had 48 hours to edit the entire film. We started editing the second we wrapped, on the plane, and eventually at our hotel in NOLA, delivering a cut to the Chief Marketing Officer (CMO) minutes before we promised.

After the screening, the CMO said, "This is amazing. We just need a stronger Call to Action and some graphics." The problem? We knew our creative director (a recent film school graduate) wanted to stay away from this direction. Ironically, the CMO's comment echoed our exact words to the creative director earlier, but he didn't want to implement these notes because he felt they might take away from the video's cinematic qualities. Trying to be impartial, I presented this idea to the CMO, attempting to protect our young creative director. "We don't want to ruin the cinematic qualities of the video by integrating graphics that might compromise the integrity of the piece." Our client looked at me like I had just spoken in tongues. Dumfounded, he abruptly replied, "We're creating a marketing video, not a film. Change it." To which I promptly responded with a smile, "Absolutely!"

This experience was one of our first pivotal learning moments. The greatest film schools in the country do a great job of educating students on work in the film industry, but few of these institutions teach their students about marketing and advertising.

Over the years, we have hired employees from some of the top film schools, including USC, AFI, and Harvard. Time and again, we have noticed one of the things they don't learn is how to tell stories from a marketing perspective. Instead, they learn storytelling emphasizing entertainment and longer format experiences. There is very little instruction on how to use video to create compelling stories selling people on brands or products.

The key to the success of any video marketing campaign is really the intersection between these two focuses: the entertaining/long-form artistic approach and the pragmatic, sales-oriented one. It's not always possible to marry these two disciplines; but when it happens, it leads to better results.

Apple is a textbook example of integrating a solid marketing plan with narrative strategy. They continually offer heart-centered stories to remind people they are offering more than just a phone. GoldieBlox, the toy company we mentioned earlier, does, too. Though they make toys, what's really unique is how their ads deliver an empowering narrative for girls wishing to one day grow up to be engineers.

Though we are talking about difficulties surrounding the hiring of film school students, similar hiring challenges apply when hiring *any* employee for your in-house team because of the nature of the job. You are not hiring a plumber or an office manager to follow orders. You need a creative-minded individual, and this can lead to challenges in management.

Some important questions to consider when hiring your team include:

- *How will I know if their work is good?*
- *How will I be sure they are properly motivated and inspired?*
- *What are their personal character traits, and can I work with them?*
- *How might I get the best output from this potential team member?*

The reason we pose these questions is because hiring film school graduates may not even be an option. We happen to live and work in Southern California, so there are plenty to hire, but what if you live elsewhere in the country? If you're trying to create an in-house team in Fargo, North Dakota, you may not have access to many film school graduates. Being cognizant of the personnel disparities from region to region, as well as outside of the US, we will summarize key employment aspects to consider when hiring.

- What is this person's experience level?
- *(Have they shot/edited anything beyond wedding videos?)*
- What equipment can they use?
- *(Do they have their own? Are they up to date on the newest technology?)*
- Do they have a reel?
- *(If they do, request samples of their work.)*
- If the candidate doesn't have the requisite capabilities, experience, or equipment, are they at

least willing to put time and effort into learning what it takes to be a good video marketer?

(This question is imperative if you're trying to turn a current marketing employee into a Preditor, for example.)

Ultimately, anyone interested in video can become quite good at marketing by continuously doing research, practicing, and acquiring an education. To aid you and your team, we also suggest you consult all of the free tutorials on our YouTube channel, youtube.com/videofort, as well as the additional resources at videofort.com/book. These are meant to teach anyone with a limited background how to become expert in this field. Yes, it certainly takes time, motivation, and energy, but improving a person's abilities can be simplified by using the resources on our site.

Like most things, perfecting an individual's abilities comes down to practice. If you have a potential employee with a limited portfolio, yet is eager to learn, it's possible to accomplish great things quickly through focused repetition. Another way to get your hire thinking the right way is to ask them to come up with creative styles they like and could replicate as a form of learning.

This can be likened to improving in sports. If you see a basketball player you admire because he's got a terrific crossover, the best thing to ask yourself is: *how can I learn to do that?* Practice. Going out on the court as much as you can will help you get there. The same idea holds true with a fledgling video marketer. Ask your person to find inspiring videos they like, then have them copy the visual style down in a sketch book to discover ways they might accomplish something similar.

Last, when it comes to determining how to manage creative personnel, we have found it's crucial to give our creative people the opportunity to be creative. It sounds so simple, but it's so important. In our experience, creative people are apprehensive of helicopter management styles. They dislike micromanagement because it gets in the way of their creative thinking.

Also, when working with our teams, we have found nothing excites them more than being given opportunities to shine. This has held especially true when providing interesting chances to be creative in new ways they've never experienced. Little things can make a big difference. We have witnessed incredible results by providing higher-end cameras or by sending them to a cool new destination they've never filmed before. Just the simple act of providing them a bit more money for set design, even if not completely necessary, brought fantastic results. Conversely, forcing creatives to complete repetitive or bland video projects can lead to decreased employee morale.

These are, of course, some small tips and tricks; the real challenge is managing a viable team day in, day out. When it comes to getting the most from your people, the best advice is to establish a consistent management style. We have been most successful with our creatives when establishing context, defining boundaries, and setting goals. And as a rule, we never micromanage. Our team needs to be able to do their own thing.

What is an Outsource Team?

The fact is, most ad agencies sub out production work. This is not necessarily a bad thing, but it is important to know when making your creative/budgetary decisions. Before we explain the implications, let's first define an outsource team. An outsource team is an outside production company or organization of some kind primarily focused on creating content.

Outsource teams can vary in makeup, from three- to four-person production shops handling smaller budgets, to full-scale production companies that also work on feature films and television shows.

Traditionally, organizations have used advertising agencies of record. These charge the client a monthly retainer for access to the agency's personnel. Benefits arise from an agency's collective nature, as well as the know-how experience of individuals engaged in marketing and advertising every single day. Using an agency also grants your organization numerous capabilities without the need to bring on in-house people.

The outsource model has surged in recent years due to the emergence of the various channels we have discussed. If you want to capture attention in the crowded, noisy digital world, focus and expertise are required. Ad agencies typically use their staffed creative teams to develop the foundational, tactical elements of a campaign, then farm the video work to production companies. Of course, ad agencies vary from company to company, but for the most part, they take a cut of the total production cost, bill for hours spent on the project, and even charge an agency fee on top of all of this.

It's important to know when pursuing the agency route how ad agencies can bloat the process. It takes time and energy to effectively communicate to the production company responsible for the content, manage the respective individuals, and oversee logistics. Be forewarned, if you take this approach, you may be adding more ingredients to the pot that don't always make the soup better. To be fair, some instances do require huge productions, but for small- to medium-sized businesses, it usually doesn't make sense to proceed this way as you're effectively parsing the budget and creative direction out to different individuals who aren't imperative to creating the content you need.

Many of our clients began by asking the question, "Why should we pay an extra 30 percent on this production, when we could just give all the resources to VideoFort and make a much better product?" Unfortunately, this put us in a sticky situation. At the time, we had a couple of strong agency relationships. Working directly with brands threatened these, as well as the agencies' bottom line. In order to mitigate this risk, whenever our agency partners brought us in on a project, all communication was structured and relayed through the agency. Direct contact with the client became a fireable offense.

A former partner of ours once said it best "This is the dumbest shit I've ever seen. It's literally taking two extra days to get feedback from the client because X (name omitted) agency isn't getting my messages to them fast enough. Look at this thread, she didn't send my email to them until 48 hours after I sent it. F— this, I'm reaching out to the client directly."

We didn't work with that agency or client again after this little break of protocol. We learned that going brand-direct worked not only for us, but for the client. We have always had strong creative and strategic skills, but customer service is also extremely important to us. I'm sure you've probably had some hit or miss experiences with production companies. Delayed responses, large change-order fees, and overpromising and under-delivering tend to be frequent in the industry. There's no easy way to vet a new production partner. It takes time, research, and trial and error to find the perfect match.

Most production companies work on a percentage basis. Whatever the budget, their profit margin is based on the percentage. The rest of the resources go to the end product itself, meaning better cameras, better crew, better talent, and ultimately better results, when working with a reputable production company. This can vary greatly from production company to production company, though, which is why you will sometimes receive vastly different quotes.

In my opinion, this model encourages production companies to include unnecessary personnel, equipment, and the like to increase the cost of the production, as well as their profit margin. Instead, we recommend working with a company where everything is included, from creative development to post production, within a predetermined budget. The only way a budget should change is if you (the client) alter the scope of work after a contract is signed. Companies who operate in this manner eliminate the unnecessary stress of budget control. It's on them to deliver what they said they were going to deliver' and if they mess up, it's on them. Their bottom line is to make it right.

How to Find the Best Production Team for You

You need a particular style of video to best promote your brand. Perhaps you have several visual styles you think would work particularly well. However, more than likely, your bailiwick is your particular product or service, not video production and distribution. Therefore, choosing an appropriate production partner can be an important business move.

You will want someone who understands your brand, communicates well, speaks your language, has the right set of skills, and can deliver the product you need in a timely fashion. In other words, you want to look for a production company in the same way you would approach working with any vendor. Find a company with the proper *experience* that offers high quality at a fair price.

When discussing experience, it's not just about how long a company has been in business. The nature of video production requires the individuals performing the work have the proper experience necessary for each unique job. Perhaps the video requires knowledge of shooting under extreme conditions: cold weather or snow, underwater videography, and desert or mountain terrain all require specialized equipment and present potential problems only a knowledgeable crew with hands-on expertise under such conditions will be able to handle. Similarly, working in third-world countries, working with children, and working with animals (wild or domestic) also all pose specific challenges requiring specialized training and background.

Knowing the factors you will be dealing with, as well as the specific challenges your production may face, can greatly help when narrowing the list of potential production partners. If price is the overriding factor in your decision about which company to work with, there is a strong chance a lack of experience will end up costing more money in the long run. Cheaper is not always better and upfront production costs are only part of the overall picture. While there is a lot to be said for saving money, the true savings only come to light when a usable, professional product has been completed, meeting your brand's needs and hopefully *exceeding your expectations.*

True, you want a company that can work within your budget. But beyond that, you should focus on finding a company with experience producing video for your type of product or service in an environment and at the scale involved in the market you are planning to impact.

Ask These Questions to any Potential Outsourced Production Company:

- Can you scale from one video or one hundred videos at the same time, if needed?
- Can you produce video in all the required deliverable formats?
- Can you produce a corporate training video that looks as good as a Hollywood movie?
- Can you produce a B2B video that looks as good as a B2C or external video?

Request a Reel and Meet in Person

You will need to see examples of your potential production partner's work on a reel demonstrating the company is capable of producing the type of videos you want to represent your brand. Look for clever and engaging messaging in their samples, and make sure that they are capable of crafting video that is fun and exciting. Modern audiences frequently have a short online attention span, with a click-through mentality. You do not want to waste their time or allow them to feel bored while watching your video, so the ability of a production company to provide content that pulls in viewers is essential.

Once you have several reels in hand you feel show the talent and technical acumen necessary to properly communicate the value of your brand, the next step is essential: meet these potential production partners in person.

Media creation is a collaborative process. You will be working closely together to ensure your brand is accurately represented and your product or service is highlighted in the most appropriate way. Getting to know your potential partners in this endeavor will go a long way toward ensuring a smooth experience with optimal results. Each production company on your short list will need to be approached in the same manner.

Begin with an interview. This is a professional business relationship, and you want to treat this one like you would a new hire for any important position within your company. What does their studio/office look like? Is it clean and organized? Are the employees well-dressed and professional or more free-spirited and creative? You will need to make sure the personality of the production company, how it does business, and how it approaches the creative process is in line with your team and your brand.

But what you really want to find out is whether they have a clear understanding of your business. Make sure they see how things look from your side of the table. No matter how talented or technically savvy a potential production partner may seem from their reel, if they cannot share completely in your vision, it is unlikely they will be able to craft content that will make a positive impact for your company.

You want a partner who will become part of the culture of your business. Ultimately, if a production partner does not fully understand what your business is about, they will be unable to communicate the proper message. This choice is about discovering the production partner capable of understanding the nuance of your brand. *You need someone to strategically communicate for you.*

What to Look for in Your Interview:

- Does this production company understand my business model?
- Can this production company communicate who and what my business is?
- Will this production company be able to maintain the tone of my brand?
- Will this production company be able to communicate both soft and hard information?

Advantages and Disadvantages of Outsourcing

Outsourcing can be beneficial as a turnkey solution. If your marketing department is stretched and you can't bring on your own in-house team without requiring significant time and effort, hiring someone skilled will allow you to create content on a per project basis. If you pick the right people, presumably they won't go over budget unless the scope of work changes.

Working with an outside entity has disadvantages, though. The thrust of this book is that it typically costs more on a per hour basis to outsource than it does to use your own in-house team. However, if you're only looking to create content two, three, or four times a year, it does make more monetary sense to outsource than build from within.

On the other hand, if you see the value of pumping out content on a regular, consistent basis to various channels for concerted brand exposure, build your own in-house team. This way you can be sure you are constantly creating quality work. The downside is management. Before you go this route, be sure your company can afford and handle the extra employees, as well as the extra workload.

Going back to the outsource model, you may find it helpful that this model gives you the benefit of experience. This team will most likely have worked on different types and styles of projects. They can also typically provide higher quality work much faster. The flipside to that, though, *is* their prolificacy. Working on so many projects can mean their creative and mental energies are not solely dedicated to your project. That's the beauty of using an in-house team. Their number one concern is your company and your goals. Such exclusive focus can bring better long-term solutions. It will also better align with your company culture, allowing you to make more content with a group of creatives 100 percent committed all the time.

Ultimately, it comes down to your budget and creative goals. With medium-sized companies, it can be smarter to outsource, especially if you're only creating content a handful of times per year. The burden to bring on, train, and implement a full-time in-house team is not worth it financially. Fortune 500 companies often put their own spin on this trend; they usually have a smaller in-house team for consistent output, and they augment their capacity several times a year with a trusted outsourced team to scale-up as needed.

Costs, Retainers, and Other Important Considerations

Costs will be contingent upon a variety of factors. We have observed through our experiences providing Requests for Proposals (RFPs) that companies frequently accept the bids of the lowest cost provider without fully understanding everything that is included. Unfortunately, they don't grasp all the ramifications of selecting based on price. In this industry, you get what you pay for. Our approach is to establish a budget with the client first, then decide on the creative possibilities. The reason for this is to allow the most accurate apples-to-apples comparison with different production companies. It is much easier than saying, "Here's the script. How much will it cost?"

The deeper rationale pertains to the new technological reality. You can shoot something with an iPhone for much less than employing a talented 10-person crew armed with great equipment. We have observed this phenomenon often enough to warrant a helpful rule of thumb. If your business's annual marketing budget is between $0 to $100,000, hire a part-time videographer in-house. If it's between $100,000 to $500,000, an outsourced production company makes sense. If your budget is over $500,000, build a robust in-house production department or create an in-house "skeleton crew" of video-makers with the intention of augmenting productions on a case-by-case basis with production companies and/or freelancers.

Our advice is backed by a lot of thinking and experience, also known as mistakes. We have discovered the smaller businesses can hire a full-time videographer, such as a recent film school graduate, for between $35,000 and $40,000 fully burdened. Then, the company can spend another $10,000 on simple equipment to use to produce content. Anytime your budget and needs exceed the individual filmmaker, you slip into the $100,000 to $500,000 range. At this point, you will notice how hiring an outsourced team can give you more bang for your buck because you can leverage more people with more experience and better equipment. This is the sweet spot for the outsourced team. Once you're spending more than $500,000 with an outsourced team, it's time to start considering bringing resources back in-house and building out your own production department. This determination should be made based on your multi-year content marketing strategy and the direction you want to take the marketing department (in-housing versus outsourcing).

Speaking of content requirements, let's address retainers. Most production companies work on a per project basis. However, if you intend to develop consistent content throughout the year, for example, two or three studio-based videos of a similar format, a retainer may be helpful. The retainer can be beneficial even if you don't have an ongoing project. Retainer-based production companies or video agencies can develop a personalized strategy for you and your team as an additional resource. It can work so they act as your own in-house team, however, without the worries involved in staffing, payroll, and insurance commensurate with having a full-time employee.

This model of a project-based approach can work especially well if you are producing four to five projects a year with a big downtime in which you don't necessarily need anyone creating video content. I recommend trying it small scale on an individual project. The second time around, consider some kind of bulk deal in which it's more than one project with a company, or a short-term retainer. Based on how the relationship goes, you can consider a longer-term retainer pertaining to a much larger quantity of projects package.

Consider it this way: it's important to date and build the relationship before tying the knot. The best way to accomplish this with a video company is always to begin with one project. Be transparent with your outsourced video company. Inform them this is a single project deal and you intend to evaluate based on how the project goes. If it works out, the door is open for a couple more projects together, and so on. This can be the best way to build the relationship. For the love of God, don't promise more projects if they do a good job or if they give you a discount on the first project. Many of our friends have been burned by this unethical practice.

How to Judge Work Quality

It's simple to determine a video product's quality. You can tell it's good if the person or team achieves the main goals you set out to achieve in the beginning. Obviously, there are also subjective differences and various organizations view content differently. For instance, we've worked with individuals over the moon with a video they showed us. Yet we can take one look at it and can instantly size it up as total garbage.

Though quality is really in the eyes of the beholder, there are practical considerations for judging output. We measure good and bad based on engagement and retention, as well as these important questions: *What is the outcome? Did you achieve the main goals you set out to achieve?* This is something we will discuss in greater detail later, but for the now, the key is to always have a strategy and be sure you have a Key Performance Indicator (KPI) in place ahead of time. This latter point is so that once a video launches, wherever you launch it, you're able to measure it effectively to determine if the results were positive or negative. These KPI's can be as simple as viewership and can get extremely detailed, including Cost Per View, Average and View Length, and/or if you really want to set high standards, something tied to conversion, such as units sold or revenues generated.

Interpersonal dealings are another crucial way to assess quality. Rule number one: your video team should be an absolute pleasure and joy to work with. When it comes to business, video production is the most fun, creative, and exciting activity you can do. It should be a blast.

Next, the people you work with need to be professionals. There can be all kinds of craziness with a shoot due to the many variables involved, such as weather, locations, and talent, but no matter what, a level of courtesy is required.

It's interesting how strange personality traits can come out on set. Some people speak well in person but blow it on camera. Your video team should be aware of these kinds of crises in the making and seek to continually keep you at ease. It's simple to recognize you are in the presence of professionals upfront; they are typically relaxed and easygoing. We like to think about it this way: when it comes down to it, filmmaking is the most playful, childlike work most people will ever experience working at a corporation, and it should feel that way: light-hearted and fun.

Even so, working professionals must also come prepared. They should know how to plan well. Potential pitfalls must be foreseen in advance. Contingency plans need to be in place. You can get a good sense of a person's readiness by the types of informed questions they ask, such as: *Will there be Wi-Fi on location? How about power? Do we need to bring our own generators? When is the best time of day to film at your location?* Also, if professionals notice inclement weather is expected for the shoot date, they will ask you if rain will compromise the desired look and feel of your video. These are little things, but they're important.

One more thing to recognize is that the creative process can be difficult. The final product should be of great quality, but like anything creative, it's hard to predict whether it will be successful. It may sound counter-intuitive to suggest this, but it doesn't matter so much if the video turns out to be as great as you hoped. What matters more is this: *did the professionals meet the previously discussed and agreed upon goals?*

The fact of the matter is sometimes outstanding teams working with terrific companies promoting excellent products still end up with an ad that doesn't resonate. It's similar to how a fantastic director can create a big budget Hollywood movie but it doesn't play well to audiences. Obviously, the director had every intention of creating a commercial film while shooting it, the film just missed the mark. The professional distinction suggests that so long as everyone was prepared, worked well together, and met the goals and deadlines, you have a great team that can be used again. Despite any hiccups or variables beyond your control, if the team met the above considerations, there is no reason you shouldn't continue working together.

For a list of questions you should ask every potential video production partner, a sample creative brief to provide to each partner, and additional production resources, go to videofort.com/book.

How to Develop and Evaluate a Request for Proposal (RFP)

The first step to creating an RFP is to consider your overall marketing strategy. Establish what type of content you need to create, your target audience, what you wish to accomplish, and as many details as you can of the project scope. Including your budget is imperative, even if it's a range or "not to exceed" amount. Frequently, companies won't put their budget in the initial RFP because they feel like they don't have the experience to know the correct figure.

Before developing an RFP, we recommend calling different production companies to get a general idea of costs. The reason is production budgets can range widely and it's not always easy to compare apples to apples if every line item in a budget isn't laid out. For instance, right now, I could shoot a 30-second 4k resolution commercial on an iPhone, charging you, let's say $100. Or I could get some A-list talent, a large crew, fancy director, top-of-line camera lighting, and grip systems and charge $5 million for a 30-second 4k resolution commercial. Bottom line: when a budget isn't provided, it creates inefficiencies, both on the side of the RFP contributor, as well as the prospective production company.

It's important to recognize that video production costs typically pertain to labor. For the most part, you are paying for a group of people's time, plus gear rental, and whatever additional materials, locations, permits, props, and the like. Budget changes primarily involve a time modification or an update in regard to materials. It's challenging to understand this from a client perspective until you are producing in-house.

Even if you don't have any creative that needs to be bid on by prospective production companies, it's still important to provide general specifications in your Request for Proposal:

- Background on the project: What is the product or service? What purpose does it serve?
- Brand Guidelines: Who is your company? What is the look and feel of your brand? Are there any examples of related work resembling your brand?

- Project Deliverables: How many videos do you need, and what are their approximate lengths? Where will the projects be distributed?
- Project Purpose: Why are you creating this project? Why do you need these videos? What are you trying to achieve with this content?
- Project Budget: What is the not-to-exceed amount? Are you looking for the lowest cost provider or highest value provider?

Conversely, if you leave things open-ended and vague, saying something to this effect: "We have an island in the Bahamas where we wish to shoot an online video, and we need to know how much it's going to cost," this can be problematic. You are not being specific enough to allow the team to create a reasonable proposal. You're also potentially opening the door for inexperienced production companies to throw low bids into the pile. Unfortunately, these companies may not have the resources needed to achieve your marketing goals. The key? By specifying variables, you will receive a better understanding of the project scope. In turn, you will receive sophisticated answers to your RFP and often end up working with a solid production partner.

When evaluating returned proposals, it's necessary to make sure the proposal contains a firm, fixed price in line with your project scope. This assures there won't be additional charges unless the scope of work changes. Line itemed AICP bids are the industry standard for higher-end productions, but at the very least, all of the production company's resources (crew, time, rentals, permits, travel, locations, talent, casting, etc.) should be provided in the proposal.

One of the reasons why we have such local clients is because prior to working with our company, they would frequently receive proposals from companies that offered a low budget option. This company would then turn around and execute the production with even fewer resources indicated in the proposal (for example, a single man production), resulting in an end product that not only looked terrible, it didn't remotely resemble the examples provided. True, they may have made good on their promise to deliver a 60-second video, but it was nowhere close to what other production companies might have done, even at a slightly higher budget. Instead, these less than scrupulous production companies made a big profit because they didn't spend much on the resources for the shoot.

To reiterate, be sure you understand what to include in the RFP submission. Be familiar with all the details, including the line items. The better production companies will provide you transparency; they will show you exactly what they are earning, their costs, and their procedure. If you've never worked with someone and need to evaluate a potential relationship, this is our biggest recommendation: be wary of any and all RFP's lacking specificity. Vagueness is the biggest red flag when it comes to evaluating potential production partners.

How to Move Forward Upon Selecting Your Team

First, it's always a good idea to reach out to the winning team right away. You need to be sure they are still comfortable with winning the RFP. The reason why is there have been instances where competing production companies underbid and when the job was awarded, they weren't able to fulfill their agreement as they didn't understand the full scope of work. If this happens, you still have the ability to go to your second choice if it doesn't work out with your primary selection.

Next, it's always a good idea to reach out to every production company that did not win the RFP. Explain to them why they didn't get the job. There are practical rationales for this recommendation. It will help them improve so in the future you do get a much better bid. Also, treating production companies professionally goes a long way, long-term. The last thing you want is to burn a production company, because if in the future your preferred incumbent isn't available, you will need to have other resources.

Initiating a kick-off call is a smart idea and a paramount step in our process. Use this conversation to re-establish your goals and objectives, starting the creative process if it hasn't begun already. Then tackle actual production logistics. Schedule the production date, learn more about the team, and be sure you understand their approach. These are things you should know already, but it's important to solidify everything submitted in the RFP.

This call is also the ideal time to discuss strategy. Quick distinction here—there can be two strategies as concerns an RFP: an RFP could be more discrete, meaning it is based on a single project, or an RFP could be created with more of a long-term goal, such as becoming a client's video agency. The latter is important because if you select an organization as your video agency, they should act as your ad agency in the sense that you will consult with them on an ongoing basis. You may work with them at any time and/or they could develop a strategy for you to pursue.

Next, the particulars need to be put into a contract. With the understanding that people's time isn't free, it would behoove all parties to establish a contract delineating something to the effect that the awarded production company (or video agency) will be respon-sible for developing part of or all of the video strategy, the marketing plan, and the creative for the content. In addition, this company will be responsible for all of the production particulars, as well as all post-pro-duction work. Bundling these responsibilities into one contract is recommended.

When it comes to strategy and moving forward, it's important to recognize anyone you hire will not know your brand as well as you do. Accordingly, you need to walk them through the entire process as if they are an infant learning to walk for the first time. There are no stupid questions; don't assume they know the intricacies of your brand, your product, or your cus-tomer. There is also no such thing as too much infor-mation. The person on the other end of the call will always benefit from you educating them. Once they better understand you and your brand, they will be more equipped to consult with you on strategy or, if you are paying them, how to develop a viable strategy on their own.

How to Be Sure You are Receiving Quality Work

As mentioned earlier, the key is to establish different Key Performance Indicators (KPI's) you can objectively measure. To be fair, we have worked without estab-lished KPI's before. The organization simply told us they wanted a video, and we created the best one we could, knowing maybe a thousand people would watch it in their group. Their main goal was narrow in focus: to get certain information across in the most exciting possible way to a select group.

A great example of this occurred with one of our clients, the multi-national real estate company I mentioned earlier. We've been working with them for nearly a decade now, practically unheard of this industry. One of the main reasons they continue working with us is our dedication to taking innovative approaches to creating content. Over the years, we have continued to create vibrant new videos that makes them seem like they're the hottest new tech company, not a 100-year-old real estate brand.

To reiterate, our approach doesn't always involve KPI's, in the form of viewership or engagement. Rather, our customer consistently requests content to get their agent base fired up and engaged with their brand. Additionally, we often make sure our original plans are executed exactly how we set out to do them. As mentioned earlier, the planning phase is extremely important. Don't be surprised if projects with a lower budget need additional resources from your team. This can come in the form of logistical planning, or it can involve your operations team. For example, if you're interviewing customers as part of a digital testimonial campaign, it may be much easier for your team to execute the discovery portion of the process: finding customers who look good and have great things to say about your brand. For some of our clients, we've leveraged real estate listings as locations and have even used the brand's team members as background "actors." This is the trade-off when it comes to budget, as these elements can add zeros to your bottom line.

Let's flip the script now and discuss what to do when things go wrong with your production team. Here is an important question: *What do you do when your production company doesn't deliver on its promises?* First, it's important to understand a video or ad agency is only as good as their last piece of work. That's what makes our industry so volatile and challenging. Yet, at the same time, this dynamic flux allows consistently good agencies to stand out. You wouldn't go back to a restaurant with bad servers and horrible food, right? Similarly, why would you go back to an ad agency that didn't deliver on your expectations?

Part of finding the right balance is encouraging a production company to understand the value of under-promising and over-delivering. This mindset can begin with the very first project. You can mostly assume good results if a production company responds to emails within two hours versus two days; tells you no and explains why; works with you on different solutions as opposed to setting up roadblocks; shows up to set on time and dressed professionally; and, most important, completes a project without any overages.

Another way to discern the quality of a production company is to ask for referrals from previous clients. You'll soon discover just how important it is to structure a contract so you're not tied up for multiple years at a time, especially if they can't deliver referrals and/or are not living up to undelivered promises. Even if a project costs less, chances are you can't negotiate an opt-out clause once a contract is signed, so always make sure everything is discussed ahead of time.

Bad things happen, even to great people. Outstanding production companies can falter when unforeseen events occur, such as a director getting sick or something expensive breaking—these things do happen—so it's not right to judge a production company based on one event. However, if you don't get a great feeling from your production company in the beginning, it's not a fun experience on set, and the quality of the product isn't stellar, then it's probably time to make a change. Just be sure to prepare for this unfortunate contingency by having a candid conversation prior to signing on the dotted line.

Now that you better understand the rationale for either in-housing versus outsourcing and what both strategies entail, let's discuss how to frame your content for maximum engagement.

CHAPTER SEVEN: Developing a Marketing Strategy: Lead from *The Why, Not The What or The How*

"The only way to do great work is to love what you do. If you haven't found it, keep looking. Don't settle."

~Steve Jobs, Entrepreneur

What is a Video Marketing Strategy?

Based on key insights and observations of your target market, a video marketing strategy is the plan dictating what you wish to achieve and accomplish. It can be likened to a comprehensive guide to all of your video content distribution or an overarching roadmap for success. Imagine you are going on a road trip from San Diego to Las Vegas. Before setting out, you need to figure out vital details: what car you are taking, when and where you intend to stop, what road to take, etc. Before ever leaving, you can refine your approach by determining not only the quickest route, but also the most efficient. How might you best circumvent traffic? Perhaps you could leave earlier or travel at a certain time to avoid rush hour? All of these variables can greatly inform the mechanics of your trip, influencing how to best get from point A to point B.

When it comes to the specifics of a quality video marketing strategy, the same preparation and guidance are needed as your roadmap. Core elements should include a target audience definition, as well as goals encompassing the intended audience takeaway.

It's also instrumental to know what type of feelings you wish to convey.

A good strategy should answer some, if not all, of these branding questions:

1. Who is your brand?
2. What message do you want to impart through your content?
3. How might your target audience react to your message?
4. Where do you wish to drive your audience?

In addition to considering these elements, there are numerous other variables that come into play when creating a single piece of content. If you want a successful video marketing campaign encompassing 10, 50, even 100 pieces of video, strategy coherence is required. To go back to the road map analogy, if any content piece isn't following the overall plan, you may run the risk of ending up at point C, instead of point B. Not only might this lead you on a completely different route, it could end up taking much longer to get there. Ultimately, the more information, research, and practical knowledge you put into your strategy, the better off you'll be in the long run.

Why It's Hard to Go Viral

A viral video can quite literally break your brand, in a good way, of course. Blowing up the view count will exponentially grow your exposure, undoubtedly helping your business. The reality, however, is going viral is hard to do. We often encounter clients wanting a cool video, something that will pop with the masses, cementing their brand in the public consciousness. This a laudable ambition, but the problem is the client often hasn't seriously considered their strategy. *What will bring a gargantuan audience? What novelty will entice people to watch their video? How are they going to get their video out to the masses?* All of these elements need to come together just right to create digital magic.

There is another reason why many brands can't just knock viral videos out of the park. To understand why, here is a brief historical context. In the early 2000's, when YouTube had just launched, viral videos were easier to create. You could seed a viral video by purchasing views and building traffic, much in the same way a snowball starts rolling downhill. If you take a ball of snow and drop it at the top of the mountain in six inches of powder, it's going to sink into the snow and stay there. However, if you give the snowball a little help and gently start rolling it down the hill, momentum is created. Before you know it, an uncontrollable sphere of snow is rocketing down the mountain.

Back then, it was simpler to come up with a unique idea no one had ever seen before and effectively spread it through social media. Flash forward a decade and the landscape has dramatically altered. Audiences are so bombarded with content, user fatigue has set in. The new bar to nail a viral video, something hitting the million-view mark organically, is much harder to achieve than it used to be.

Another reason why going viral is so challenging is the current zeitgeist demands so much more from creators. More components are required to create a viral today because consumers have been desensitized. They know the game when it comes to video, especially branded content. The sheer volume of media has sharpened their tastes, making audiences more sophisticated and picky. They don't want to be sold to. They can see right through marketing shlock. They prefer authentic content: something real, emotional, different, unique. If you want the masses to watch your content, please bear this in mind. Now, let's look at a recent campaign to see how it's done right.

Dove: Drawing Fire with Authenticity

Dove's Real Beauty Campaign represents what's possible when authenticity is utilized to maximize virality. Their ad team told an effective story by presenting a *Cause Marketing* approach to sell their products. What happened was Dove recruited an actual FBI-trained forensic artist to draw composite sketches of women based on their own descriptions of their facial features. These females couldn't help but reveal all the negative things other people had said about them. For instance, one woman said, "I have a fat, rounder face." Another lady said, "My mom told me I had a big jaw."

In an interesting twist, the women had been asked to spend time with strangers. Neither the women nor the strangers were told why. Later, the sketch artist asked the strangers to describe these same women. He asked them questions, such as: "What do you think of this person? Could you describe her looks?" When the completed drawings appeared side-by-side, the women were flabbergasted. The campaign demonstrated its tagline through the raw, visceral reactions of the surprised women. 'You are more beautiful than you think.'

This video rang out far and wide on the Internet because it tapped into something emotional in both the subjects and the viewers. It's no secret we live in a society prone to objectifying women based on their looks. As a result, many of them feel insecure about the way they are perceived. An ad positively affirming all women, showing them they are for more beautiful than what they have been led to believe is highly sharable. Authentic, engaging, and highly emotional, this video resonated with audiences because the women recognized the truth: they saw themselves as uglier than the world ever did. Dove aptly demonstrated how real beauty comes from within, winning fans and converts.

Now that we understand why Dove's campaign worked so well as a vibrant Internet meme, let's reverse engineer the process to understand how they pulled this feat off. There are numerous ways to create viral videos from a brand perspective, but it's so much harder; you really need to dig deep. Instead, let's consider it from a content perspective. Most likely, the idea began in a room of creatives. They probably began this ad thinking about their goal: to bring Dove to life through innovative ways beyond their previous ads picturing milk pouring into a bar of soap.

Someone in this meeting must have said, "Now, how can we break this? What's going on with our target audience we can tap into?" Someone else may have identified their customers' pain point: many women suffer from low self-esteem. They don't see themselves in the best possible light, especially with the fashion industry gearing so much content toward making women feel inadequate in order to sell them more skincare products and beauty items.

The core insight was to counter such a negative message; rather than cudgel women into purchasing more items to stave off feelings of inadequacy due to their looks, they empowered women to recognize their own self-worth. Through meaningful stories featuring women experientially feeling honest emotions, viewers received a different, uplifting idea: they are far more beautiful than they think.

In retrospect, it may sound cynical to pick apart how these marketers brought such noble sentiment to fruition, but it's highly instructive for our purposes. Back in this creative meeting, probably 10 to 15 ideas were brought forward to execute this strategy once it was decided upon. Then finally, someone hit pay dirt. "What if we drew what other people see, rather than what the women view as themselves?"

From this breakthrough, an ingenious video campaign was born. Dove has been running this ad for several years now. Each time they launch a new iteration, they captivate audiences because they wisely cling to their key insights on female empowerment, emotional truth, and story. The videos continue to be received well due to their authenticity. These commercials stand out because they are infused with meaning. It's far easier to share a narrative genuinely pulling on the heart strings than something you can tell was made to pedal some product through lies or deception.

There's an old saying in Silicon Valley that "all marketers are liars," as exemplified by Seth Godin's eponymous book. Millennials, in particular, get this intuitively and, therefore, shut out anything smacking of deceit, avoiding TV commercials in favor of on-demand content via platforms, like Netflix. Bottom line: companies like Dove continue to get it right because they understand authenticity and storytelling are imperative to break through to their audience. The above campaign offers an illustrative example of what will be required to make an impact in the future. To create an ad with any hope of going viral, you need authenticity, a good story, and a clever way to connect with your target audience.

Apple and The Golden Circle Philosophy

To go further in understanding how brands can res-onate with audiences, let's review the Golden Circle Philosophy. This idea comes from author and market-ing consultant Simon Sinek, offering insight into how people and brands communicate. Sinek puts forward a naturally occurring pattern constructed of three el-ements comprising rings of a circle: *The What, The How, and The Why.*

The farthest outside ring, *The What,* is the simplest and easiest to identify. Every person on Earth knows what they do. They know their titles, their function, the products they sell or the services they offer. Take Dell. They sell computers and tech products. That's their *What.*

When it comes to *The How,* the middle ring, some people know how they do it. *The How* includes actual things people do to differentiate themselves from their peers as special. Not as obvious as *The What,* the an-swer to this may be found in edifying questions, such as: "How do you provide real value to your clients?" or "How do you do manage your time?"

The Why, located in the circle's center, is the hard-est item to grasp. It's not about making money; that's the result. *The Why* is the purpose, cause, or belief: the very reason you exist. Not necessarily a function of what you're doing or how you're doing it, *The Why* is your raison d'être, the underlying reasoning behind your organization.

Understanding your *Why* provides you with clari-ty, meaning, and direction. A mechanism to filter your decisions, it brings your cause to life. For instance, when you begin considering everything through the lens, "Is this part of my *Why?* Is this really my purpose as a brand?", it will instill each conversation with tremendous focus, far beyond simply understanding *The What* and *The How.*

Before we examine Apple's marketing approach in light of this context, let's unpack this concept a bit more. Sinek's concept matters when it comes to designing viral marketing campaigns that resonate with audiences due to the way our brains function. There are two different parts of the brain, the limbic and neocortex. The neocortex filters out the crap; it measures worth and value in terms of rational features and benefits. The limbic, on the other hand, governs our emotions. It determines how we *feel* about something, such as a brand.

Apple commands brand loyalty, says Sinek in an influential Ted Talk (search Simon Sinek on ted.com), precisely because it leads with emotion. Apple taps into the *Why,* before *The What* and *The How.* Just as Dove uses compelling stories to connect with hearts and minds, Apple continues to make audiences feel something about its brand.

Apple wins over converts, not simply because of its products' features and benefits, but because of its purpose-driven narrative. Again and again, Apple connects with users, convincing people to believe their brand exists to make their lives easier. Following suit with their *What* and *How,* they also deliver on that momentum by creating exceptional products.

As we have seen, video marketing works best with a roadmap or strategy. The content strategy driving Apple's video campaign is informed by their *Why-centered* ethos. Fundamentally changing the typical direction of video marketing, it leads with its core purpose. That purpose, that *Why* can be summarized this way:

progressiveness centered around the development of human potential through technology. Or, "We believe in thinking differently. We believe we can make the world a better place through creating products simple to use, easy to manage, and beautifully designed."

Once customers get behind Apple's *Why*, the stage is set to lead into their *How:* the sleek manner in which they market to consumers through app-based software, as well as cutting-edge retail stores. Last, but certainly not least, pertains to their *What*: Apple's products and services. Now that you're in love with Apple's philosophy and their approach through video marketing, it is easy to buy into their innovative computers, phones, and tablets.

On the flip side to this approach is Dell. Dell creates good computers for cheap. How do they do it? They manufacture and outsource from thousands of different vendors around the world to bring you a well-made machine. Their messaging strategy is the inverse of Apple, stemming from *The What*, proceeding to *The How*, then *The Why*.

This approach has worked modestly well for Dell, but they still have a fraction of the brand loyalty that Apple commands. They've tied their existence to a cost, instead of emotion. It is easy to see how Dell's strategy and messaging approach might fail with other companies, especially when you observe in most prevalent marketing and advertising messaging, you're bombarded with features, benefits, and costs—none of which position an organization's *Why*, their purpose, at the forefront of their story.

We have talked about how the limbic system helps consumers with decision making. Too often when communicating with just *The What*, video marketing that relies on promoting features and benefits gets tuned out by bullshit filters. Similarly, goodwill earned from a video communicating its *Why* can be undermined by the interjection of a logo at an inopportune time . This disruption kills the narrative's magical spell, putting off potential customers. "Oh, it's just a branded thing," a customer might say to ourselves at this point. "Turn it off!"

An Integrated, Award-Winning Strategy

Ultimately, with any created content, you're not trying to sell just one product. As the Apple example illustrates, when you're really communicating on a nonbrand level about your purpose, it sways the emotionally-based limbic brain. Forget pointing out all the features and benefits, audiences have already climbed on board with your authentic messaging. Consequently, the most effective marketing strategies are those aiming to build a lifelong consumer relationship. Falling in love with your brand can lead to far more than just discrete, one-off results.

You can witness this distinction amongst various Kickstarter campaigns. Many startups seek to impact the world, change your life, and make things easier for you. The funded campaigns typically succeed when conveying their *Why* in their initial marketing, as opposed to those who simply say something like, "This product will wash your dog faster!" This is not to say some of those brands won't succeed. If you are actually providing something faster, better, and cheaper, then great. However, what we wish to discuss is the importance of building *long-term* customer value: how to be perceived as a thought leader, a knowledge resource, and ultimately the best product or service provider in the marketplace.

In order to do that, you must intimately know your *Why*. You need to focus on it, and the core messaging needs to be consistent throughout any created content, powerfully reflecting your purpose. Even if your marketing is comedic or wacky in tone, you still need to be authentic to your core value. The key is never getting away from that.

Let's consider a campaign we created for a multi-national real estate brand as an illustration of an integrated, award-winning strategy based on all the concepts discussed so far: having a road map, being authentic, delivering emotional narrative, and delivering on the *Why*.

Our road map or strategy began with understanding our target audience.

Our client had a problem. As a hundred-year-old brand, they were not perceived as fun and exciting to customers or potential customers. There was a time when real estate was often considered more of a retirement job. Rarely did young people come out of college saying, "I want to be a real estate agent." Rightly or wrongly, the perception of a real estate agent was usually a woman in her 40s who wouldn't stop talking to you about buying a new home.

Our client wanted to crush this stereotype, while reinventing themselves as a forward-thinking, technologically-advanced brand. Though they had been around for more than a century, they were constantly innovating and their goal was to obtain more real estate agents. They specifically wanted to bring in fresh new people with passion, drive, and focus. Their ideal candidates knew the world of social media and understood technology and mobile devices.

They hired our company to execute a recruiting campaign. Now, anytime you're developing a recruiting campaign, especially when interviewing people, there's a standard way of creating said corporate video. We didn't want to do that. We wanted to showcase our client's brand in a much younger, positive, and forward-thinking light.

In order to accomplish this, we highlighted several real estate agents who were fundamentally doing things differently. We showed how they used social media to communicate with their clients, promote their properties, and interact with prospects. This is common practice now, but in 2010, this was a groundbreaking tactic few implemented.

Capitalizing on our client's *Why*: "We believe in home and all the magical things that come with it. Our calling in life is to find the one that's perfect for our clients," we spotlighted these individuals through emotionally-charged narratives, utilizing a Hollywood approach with jibs, drone footage, stirring music, and an unprecedented editing style for real estate.

This great experience helped catapult our client to create more content of a similar essence, not only stylistically, but also from a general energy standpoint. We began producing videos for their global conference, making their executive team look more like Hollywood actors than corporate suits, and their agents responded with elation. Our underlying strategy from the beginning was to create content outside of the corporate style, and it worked. As mentioned earlier, we've been working with this brand for almost a decade now, which is unheard of in our industry. Our commitment to innovation, storytelling, and starting from the *why* have all been imperative to not only our success, but the success of our client, as well.

More Exemplars of the Golden Circle Strategy

There are many insurance commercials out there. If you have watched television in the last 20 years, chances are you have been inundated with ads from Geico, State Farm, and Farmers Insurance. However, the commercials with a real purpose-driven resonance come from Esurance. Esurance's *Why* is this core principle: "We believe that technology-based insurance is more effective and efficient, and it's our mission to pass those cost savings to our clients, without sacrificing on quality."

Esurance is also interesting because the company manages to say something fundamentally different within the insurance space. Similar to our real estate client, Esurance provides a purpose-driven narrative to attract converts. Their *Why* hooks you in: technology is the new mechanism to make this industry more efficient. Esurance accomplishes its *How* through their *Why* by offering consumers products and services without the middleman, markets, fees, and sometimes needless agents. Their messaging is spot-on for millennials who don't care about having an insurance broker or agent because they don't see the value in it. Their *How* speaks to the utilization of technology to create a product that does exactly what you need for a cheaper cost. Apples to apples, they're one of the most cost-effective insurance companies, backing up their claim and continuously reinforcing the fact they're a tech-based organization providing great benefits.

Let's switch gears here and consider how this approach might work for a hypothetical company in the auto industry. Imagine you have an auto dealership. Many auto dealerships abound. It's largely a commodity-based industry; for the most part, everyone sells the same cars. Therefore, determining your *Why* message and distributing content reflecting your philosophy can really set you apart. However, this goal can be hard to achieve when cutting through so much noise. What can you say you offer? Maybe it's good customer service and a great financing program. Whatever your features and benefits, it's still more important to impart *why* you started your dealership in the first place, why your employees go to work every day, and why your return customers keep coming back.

For demonstrative purposes, let's compare two fictional dealerships' "whys." Carter Honda and Drake Honda are both based in San Diego, CA, a steady and hot market when it comes to auto sales. Given that the dealerships are only 15 miles away from each other, customers don't have a problem commuting to either if they feel they're going to receive the best value. Carter Honda focuses on long-term customer value. The dealership's owner is young, ambitious, and wants to build an evergreen brand amongst customers who return every 2 to 3 years to purchase another vehicle. He loves it when someone drives off the lot smiling from ear to ear, because that's the feeling he experienced when he purchased his first vehicle (this moment was also the catalyst for him to enter the industry).

Drake Honda's owner, on the other hand, is aggressive and focused on the bottom line. He used to be a salesman on the floor before opening Drake Honda and lives for closing deals. He could care less about what happens after the contract is signed and the customer drives off the lot. If you come into Drake Honda for a Honda Fit, their sales team will push hard to get you into an Accord. They are the car dealership that you think of when someone mentions "Car Salesman."

It's, therefore, little wonder that Drake Honda has been lagging in sales recently. The owner is panicked, and everyone is on edge. Their sales staff blames the lack of leads and foot traffic coming through the door, so the owner takes it upon himself to create a TV ad. Enlisting the assistance of the local cable station who cuts him a deal to produce the commercial free for buying air time, the owner gets in front of the camera with a script he wrote himself. "We have the best selection, the cheapest prices, and will get you in a new Honda faster than anyone! Inventory on the new 2017's is going fast, so don't wait, come in now and let us help you find a Honda that's perfect for you." As the owner speaks, B-Roll footage provided by Honda Corporate mixes over his audio. Meanwhile, a couple of shots of the dealership round out the spot.

Meanwhile, Carter Honda and his marketing team hold a meeting to formally develop their *Why*: "We believe that a car is more than a method of transportation. It's an extension of who our customers are, what they do, and where they go. It's our passion to find our customers the Honda that will become an integral part of their lives." Perhaps there is room to finesse this *Why*, but for the most part, they believe it accurately depicts how their company operates, how their sales and customer service teams handle customers, and what they really feel about their business. They even take it to the next level by laying off members of the sales and customer service staff who they feel don't embody this *Why*.

Since Carter Honda is suffering from the same sales dip as Drake Honda, its owner also decides to convey their *Why* by hiring a production company to create a series of videos highlighting return customers. Instead of focusing on the car-buying experience, their prices, or their selection, they focus on the customer's car, the experiences they've had in it, and why they love it. The customers they select are individuals who weren't sure what they wanted until the helpful staff at Carter Honda put them in a vehicle befitting their budget and needs. Featuring real customers telling real stories, these interviews are edited into dozens of variations, posted throughout social media, and even cut into a 30-second broadcast TV commercial.

Which company do you think would see consistent growth and return business?

Understandably, a car dealership's production budget can warrant a "two-hour shoot." However, the long-term negative consequences in today's digital ecosystem are far greater if the cheap content you create only focuses on undifferentiated elements, such as price, speed, and selection. Instead, the content you create should have elements of your *Why* whenever possible.

Final Thoughts on Budgeting

After you've developed your video marketing strategy based on all the above, it's time to determine a budget. It's important to be specific about how much money to invest into creating content throughout the year. Be advised your budget will be informed by the content you wish to create, your audience, how to best communicate your message, and, of course, your *Why*. Other items to consider include production and distribution.

Please go to videofort.com/book for additional materials, including an example editorial calendar and a worksheet explaining costs and workflow to create your own sample budget. Now that you understand the kinds of content you need to create to best connect with your audience, let's go into greater detail as to what makes for a winning creative team best suited to execute your vision.

CHAPTER EIGHT: How to Develop a Winning Video Marketing Team

"Many ideas grow better when transplanted into another mind than the one where they sprang up."

Oliver Wendell Holmes, Supreme Court Justice

Get Your People Involved

Developing a winning video marketing team comes down to finding individuals passionate about creating content. It also requires utilizing the best experts your location and resources can supply. As mentioned in chapter five, these folks need to have a strong foundation in marketing. A film school background can be a nice plus, but if the people you bring on don't know much about advertising, getting them up to speed is imperative in order to create effective content.

You don't necessarily want to just create content. You need specific and focused video material to help build your brand, reinforce customer relationships, and ultimately increase your organization's value by selling more products or services. A good team can be hard to find, but once you possess a crew that's a good culture fit, skilled in their abilities, and can handle projects, they should be able to work on their own without needing babysitting.

Engendering such autonomy requires integral conversations amongst all parties. Anytime you are developing an overall strategy, your team absolutely needs to be involved, especially during preliminary discussions. These will inform the type of content you need to create, drive your distribution, and determine how frequently you need to produce.

If you don't have a good idea how long the project will take and how much it will cost, the conversation and generated ideas could be a waste of time, especially if your team isn't involved in the overall strategy. To that end, some marketers don't have a lot of experience with digital video. Your team should be experts in creating content to engage with your customers in a thoughtful, pragmatic way. It's wasteful to come up with great ideas too costly to execute or that will take too long to produce.

Avoid Overwhelming Your Team from the Beginning

Involving team members early on will help maintain a consistent message throughout the year. Get them up to speed from the outset and request their insight and feedback. Most in-house teams we've worked with simply don't have the resources to fulfill all of their organization's video requests. This typically happens when resources aren't being managed appropriately. This comes from lack of coordination; the CEO, the CMO, and maybe even the COO all have different video needs. All too often, they also don't stress enough importance as to one video over the others; instead they give differing requests to the team, such as, "We need this as soon as possible." There's also the misconception that since you have an in-house team, they should be able to get everything your company needs without outsourcing any of the requests.

The problem here is an unmanaged team can quickly get overwhelmed, unable to produce content effectively because of various requests and scant leadership. From a marketing perspective, your marketing content, meant to drive sales and acquire new business, can't get produced because priorities get scrambled. Rather than creating hub, hero, or hygiene content to help grow business right away, the marketing team can get bogged down generating time-consuming and low-priority videos.

The secret to prevent this needless confusion is to put a production calendar in place at the beginning of the year. This way, everyone understands the video needs. Requests get subsequently put into a working document, allowing for a smooth production schedule. Ensuring efficiency, this prevents numerous projects from stacking up at one time and leads to better content because it's not being rushed out the door. (We've frequently seen this phenomenon with nearly every in-house team we've worked with or spoken to. Though continually receiving requests for content, many videos may not be worth creating in the grand scheme of things.)

For an example of a working production calendar, go to videofort.com/book.

Defining an Average Workload

An average workload definition depends on your team's skill level, the amount of resources at their disposal, and the type of content being created. It's certainly possible to produce 300 to 1,000 simple videos in a year with a 3-person team. If you have access to a studio or an area that could be converted to a studio and your team produces 10 videos a day, editing the content simultaneously, you can produce volumes of content. Then again, being this prolific requires real strategy considerations. It's worth asking what you're trying to achieve. Pumping out 1,000 talking head videos may not make much sense if you're only getting 100 views with little amount of engagement.

Ultimately, the average workload can vary from team to team and organization to organization. It's highly subjective, depending on the people, the organization, and the type of content being created. Rather than setting hard and fast output parameters, it's valuable to obtain constant feedback from the production team. Utilizing this information allows managers and team members to better assess when people are performing well and when they are rushing or working late nights to keep up.

It should go without saying, but it's a bad idea to burn out your team. They simply won't generate quality videos when their focus and attention to detail is overshadowed by excessive time demands. Additionally, an overstretched or overworked team can be supplemented with "hired-gun" type independent contractors to produce more content. For example, a part-time editor or a director can be a handy way to leverage your team to more efficiently create better content if your budget allows. For a look at general guidelines as to how much these individuals cost in various areas, go to videofort.com/book.

How to Keep Your Team Happy, Motivated, and On Track

We touched on something similar in chapter five regarding the mindset of creatives performing video work. It's crucial to understand the types of individuals generating great content are inventive, visionary people, but they may not always be so business savvy. The predominant reason they're in this industry is they love making content and telling stories. It's fortunate for them because, unlike say an accountant or someone who may have fallen into their profession for economic reasons, they aren't just doing it for a paycheck.

Typically, the people we work with, especially the good ones, go out and shoot on the weekend because they adore what they do. They're constantly shooting. They're constantly editing. And they're constantly looking for more stories to tell because it's their passion. Many of these creatives have higher aspirations to be a Hollywood feature film director, for example.

Keeping those intentions in mind, one of the best ways to retain talent is to let them use their creativity as mentioned earlier. The other way to not waste their abilities is to avoid assigning them overly corporate content or boring but necessary things most creatives don't relish, like HR training videos (nothing against video content for the operations departments, but let's be real ... It's where creatives go to die). Understanding the need to flex their creative muscles is key to obtaining the best results from your in-house team. If possible, encourage them to find interesting ways to make even these HR videos more fun and exciting by taking an unusual creative approach. Creative people vibe off novelty; empowering them to use their unique personalities and skills to do fun and different things can give everyone involved a lot of pleasure.

Fail to recognize this truth at your peril. It's happened to us. We lost employees who didn't want to work on corporate content anymore. They chose to do documentary or film work that inspired them. Of course, this is totally understandable in the grand scheme of things; no organization is exempt from having employees leave for greener pastures or to pursue their passions.

However, receiving constant feedback and understanding your creatives' ambitions can be a huge time-saver, especially if you truly value their work. A happy medium can be arranged when you find the right person by allowing them to head off for a couple of months to pursue their own passion projects. At the end of the day, it's all about finding the ideal balance between satisfying your creatives' need to express themselves while establishing a feasible, working production system.

Enable Your Team to Best Execute Your Vision and Strategy

Every video production requires a step-by-step process and procedure from the creative development all the way through to post-production. Pre-production is one of the most important areas to concentrate on to be certain the intended content is on brand and on strategy. How to gauge this is by ensuring the marketing team works with the video team, putting a process in place to approve creative before it is shot.

It's paramount that what your team says it's going to produce, shoot, and edit is actually what is produced, shot, and edited. Occasionally, adjustments are required. Certain barriers can prevent you from creating exactly what's in the storyboard. However, the pre-production approval process can assist in helping you understand what's needed to be sure all content is aligned with your vision. Also, as we have discussed, integrating your team into strategy sessions and discussions from the outset allows for greater communication. When everyone is privy to the same information, they are all better equipped to work together.

For the most part, success comes down to coordinating the various elements, people, and resources. Developing your video strategy comes down to figuring out who you are and what you're going to do, as well as the underlying content theme you'll create throughout the year.

Actually, executing individual videos one-by-one can be harder to do, but applying the step-by-step creative processes contained at videofort.com/book to each individual project can be hugely beneficial. Considerations include such items as knowing your target audience, your goals, your ideal customer persona, where you're going to distribute your video, and who is going to see it. Knowing this information before shooting will make things infinitely easier to manage.

Though each project is different, in general, it's important to establish your desired aesthetic. Determining your style or end guide will allow you to be sure you stay within the bounds of your brand guidelines, such as the approved language, colors, and fonts. In general, having brand guidelines will also give you a kind of creative template, both for yourself, and your team. The key is to not allow your creative to vary from the set plan. Breaking the rules can lead to problems.

But Going Off Brand Can Be a Good Thing, Right?

Deviating from a brand message can bring mixed results. Sometimes it works out well; other times it doesn't. It depends on the creativity involved. As discussed previously, there are times when somebody, usually the CMO, sets boundaries for the video team. If it's a smaller business, it can be the CEO. He or she will say, "Here's our box. Let's not veer outside of it."

Our preference is to give people the opportunity to create a couple of ideas within the box, but then also leave room for deviation. If team members come up with one to three things outside the established parameters, we like to present those, as well. The beautiful thing about the Internet and the free distribution platform is it allows us to screw up occasionally. We can produce something not very good, test it, then revise and repost it.

It's not like the 1990's where you create a TV commercial and if it doesn't work, you just wasted millions of dollars. The web allows for an ever-flowing environment where it's possible to create multiple content variations to determine which one engages the most, getting the lowest cost per thousand impressions (CPM). Running these kinds of tests will allow you to smartly revise and relaunch.

Ultimately, the Internet audience is forgiving and forgetful. As a result, you can experiment until you figure out what works best. Even so, most brands are still not okay with playing so fast and loose to their own detriment. In chapter twelve, we will explore this reluctance in greater detail, but for now it should be said this a big reason most companies are dramatically losing brand equity. For instance, 95 percent of Fortune 500s have lost market share as overrated incumbents refuse to take imaginative leaps.

All of these "startups" coming out of the woodwork with evaluations are leveraging audiences, both forgiving and forgetful, nimbly testing ideas and relaunching their products in a Kickstarter fashion. This seemingly gutsier approach has minimal risk and offers huge returns. Established brands ought to take note, but many don't. Ultimately, it will be difficult to emulate such success unless complacent organizations fundamentally change how they operate.

How to Obtain More Views and Audience Engagement

The best advice is to create better content for the end user. There are many ways to offer value. For instance, there's educational or information value, entertainment value, and even emotional value. One of the easier ways to gain eyeballs and captivate audiences is to personify a brand through fictional characters or real-life individuals. Think: Richard Branson's hot air balloon stunt.

It's difficult to market a brand without a direct personality and yet have that brand embody an idea or set of beliefs or emotions. This latter route is much harder, but when successfully accomplished, it can allow your brand to transcend time or trends. Nike does it well with their slogan, "Just do it." Coca-Cola pulls it off because people connect with Coke as being a happy brand. Coke doesn't have an individual spokesperson running around; you don't see Celine Dion and think, "Oh, that's Coca-Cola," as we might with other brands.

Those brands that do personify with a character or individual employ specific tactics to make it work. It's certainly a lot easier than trying to attach a brand to an idea or an emotion. Steve Jobs represents Apple; and though he is gone, Apple is still Apple. The company's identity didn't just go away when he passed. Even so, tying yourself to a celebrity, a figurehead, or an actor can be dangerous long-term for a variety of reasons. Employing this strategy must depend on your main goals, but be wary of linking your brand to a figure, especially a real-life one, when the potential exists for problems to arise.

Ultimately, gaining distribution success comes down to ensuring your strategy is on point and finding a good team to accomplish your vision. Again, we remind you to establish KPI's, goals, and objectives and continuously find ways to achieve them. One way is to hold your team accountable.

Developing a production schedule and rules for creative approval matter. You can't just let your team run wild and hope they come back with great stuff. Results require answerable people. Continuous and consistent mentoring must happen through communication, not in a vacuum. The creative process is perpetually honed through continuous feedback; through checking in, establishing benchmarks, and responding to what works and what doesn't. This is the optimal way to achieve better results in the long run.

What to Do When a Campaign Ends

Easy. Press the refresh button. It's a continuous circle. If you look at any process of improvement, whether it's Six Sigma or Kaizen, the key elements of the core theory suggest the work be tested and reevaluated. Upon completion, check and see what you did right and wrong. Measure the results, refine your strategy, and relaunch. Only by observing what worked and what didn't, then attempting to make it better through variations, can you truly improve. One other helpful tip is to use an After-Action Review (AAR) at the end of a campaign. Go to videofort.com/book for a template. This is a good way to establish a brief for a new campaign or to relaunch the same one.

What to Focus on When Content Demands are Low

There should never be a time when content demands are low. It can be that you don't have any events to promote in the near future, but in today's highly competitive marketplace, there will perpetually continue to be a high demand for more content. Similar to the above AAR, it can be effective to use any down time between big events or launches to revise strategies, measure, and see what's happening in order to develop more creative for future videos.

The important thing to remember is there is always something to do in the video world. Beyond actual content creation, there are other vital tasks to accomplish. "Spare time" can be used more effectively to distribute content, or more important, scout out the competition. Research what they are doing to better develop new ideas. Then start all over again.

We just covered how to put a winning team in place for best results, now let's discuss the actual content to be created in greater depth.

CHAPTER NINE: The Kaizen Approach to Fine-Tuning Your Content

"Be so good they can't ignore you."

~Steve Martin

Defining Quality Content

It's tough to determine what's good or not. *What is beauty? What is quality?* These opinions are always going to be in the eyes of the beholder. Typically, at VideoFort, we measure quality through more quantifiable metrics: actual engagement and earned media are two important KPI's we value. We study reactions. *How long do people watch the video? Do they like it? Are they sharing it? Are viewers commenting on it?*

Not too long ago, we teamed up with an international container company and their ad agency to help market a new product, a jam maker. This cooking device allows you to create homemade jam within 30 minutes as opposed to the old-school, highly time-consuming way. It also takes the hard work out of the process. Rather than bending over a pot for long stretches of time and stirring, it produces jam quickly and efficiently; you just drop in ingredients and press a button.

The product's supposed target market was hipster millennials, individuals who weren't really making jam but were more into the craft jam scene. (This was the ad agency's key insight driving them to believe millennial women would like this product because it was so simple to make.) We went to Los Angeles to create a direct response commercial, basically a quasi-infomercial. Featuring young men and women in their late 20s to early 30s, it showed them walking up as if they were coming off the street. Then they made jam by themselves right in front of the camera on a beautiful sunny day.

The spot turned out really well, terrific in fact. It was a great video, but when we launched it on TV, it turned out that older folks—baby boomers and the silent generation—were ten times more likely to buy units than a millennial. It turns out that the data and insights previously gathered by the brand were wrong. It's true, this device does make it a lot easier to make jam and jellies. However, it wasn't enough to persuade millennials to get into the craft. They would much rather buy it off the shelf.

Even though the key insight was wrong, the ad resonated with an older generation who saw these young kids making jam and said, "Oh, I could do that, too." The video became a huge commercial success, even though our original target, millennials, never responded to it. This suggests defining quality is a complex undertaking; it involves context, as well as many other different variables. Such ambiguity leads us to believe the most telling results may be measured through sharing engagement, digital landscape commenting, units sold, and the return of investment (ROI). Ultimately, of course, revenue and sold units indicated our efforts.

Content Video Marketing Versus Interruptive Video Marketing

What's the difference between interruptive video marketing and content video marketing? Though we first discussed content marketing in chapter one, it's now highly instructive to delve deeper, specifically comparing it to its opposite: interruptive marketing.

By its very nature, interruptive video marketing *disturbs*. It disrupts whatever you are doing. Prior to TIVO and the Internet age, there were few ways to avoid intrusive marketing, such as the TV commercial. You had to suffer through ads interrupting your favorite shows or change the channel. These commercials worked, of course, (remember Wendy's "Where's the beef campaign?) but there was a downside—they annoyed audiences to convey their message.

The distinction between these two methods highlights their differences and advantages. Content video marketing's supreme benefit is its utility. If you are making quality entertainment content while providing value to others, audiences will seek your content versus being disrupted by it. Instead of hounding audiences, viewers will seek and connect with your content, because they are eager to see it. They *need* your value-driven or entertainment content to solve their problems, whether it be segments explaining how to best apply concealer makeup or a group of extreme athletes jumping out of a perfectly good airplane.

It easy to see why content marketing can be a hundred times more effective than being forced to watch something. It goes back to how humans communicate and, of course, Simon Sinek's principals behind the Golden Circle's *What*, *How*, and *Why*. Our brains inherently put a block up to shield us from wasting our time, hearing things that aren't true, or being asked to believe information unrelated to our core values. Unless they are watching a really engaging, really entertaining, or fun commercial, it's hard for consumers to pay attention to interruptive video marketing because they know they're being forced to watch it.

As we have mentioned quite often in this book, one of the Internet's chief benefits is the open platform model it provides. It fosters a tremendous capacity to connect with audiences craving content. Those who successfully gain our attention do so because they create content users are interested in: content marketing.

We also know in today's digital landscape and on TV there is a constant battle for eyeballs. Consider Snapchat. The reason the company is valued so unbelievably high at present is not because they're bringing in the dough. It is because they have people's attention. It is this attention that is the currency of the Internet. If you're not connecting with audiences and people aren't seeking out your content, your message isn't being received.

The Key to Creating Engaging Content

Growing a community is paramount. It leads to subscribers, shares, and likes. We have already demonstrated the difficulty in going viral. Rather than focusing on trying to get something that will blow up, it's far better to look for ways to entertain your audience or interest them on a consistent basis.

If your product or service is less than exciting, such as insurance (no offense to any insurance marketers reading this ... although let's be honest, insurance is boring), it's important to still find novel ways to connect with users. This can be best achieved by trying to think like them. Try to imagine what they are looking for, what they need, or what bugs them. These are your customers' pain points. Diagnosing them can be a helpful first step when crafting content. Once you know what's ailing them, you can tailor a strategy to address and solve their problems in a fun, engaging, or interesting way, positioning you as an expert to be trusted.

Striking the correct balance between informative versus entertaining content often comes down to the Hub, Hero, or Hygiene strategy. Often requiring a bigger production budget and slicker production quality, hero content is meant to appeal to a mass audience. As its name suggests, it's about going big and attracting as much viewership as possible. This can happen by disrupting, inspiring, and, of course, entertaining.

Hub videos are intended to keep an audience returning to your channel on a regular basis, for instance, a product's verticalized content. Hosted vlogs, a weekly series, highlighting topics relating to your brand, or even behind-the-scenes videos can work well as hub content. These videos are also meant to primarily connect with your existing customers: individuals who have passed the awareness stage. Content should be produced at least bi-weekly and at scheduled times or days, to develop a consistent process with your viewers.

Hygiene content is more informative or "evergreen," something with long-lasting permanence. "How to" and searchable content falls into this category. People will continually need to know things such as, "How can I improve my credit?" To meet that need, a hygiene video can present effective tips and strategies invariably useful and in demand.

Balancing all three types of videos is the best way to formulate an effective marketing approach. Recognizing the need for all three types of videos while utilizing the proper one for your brand's needs will lead to the best results. For instance, a funny hero video can bring in a burst of attention but may not always be relevant; it may feature a parody of a topical news story about the election that may not be entertaining five years later.

Informative content, on the other hand, while not so incendiary or exciting, can possess a longer shelf life. At the end of the day, it comes down to your company's goals: what will bring you the most exposure and perceived value to your audience at various times based on their interests and needs.

Micro and Macro Approaches to Messaging

Different types of industries warrant various video styles. For example, elements of a "talking-head" style format may make more sense when projecting an aura of confidence and professionalism as befits a mortgage brokerage.

From a micro approach, there are few truly original ideas. If you own a mortgage company and wish to target consumers in San Diego and La Jolla, creating content highly specific to these individuals alone at the outset can be a good way to build your audience with a smaller group and expand from there.

It is far more challenging to create a successful general approach; attempting to appeal to a wide swath of the national mortgage market is considerably tougher. Wanting to be the next Barbara Corcoran requires significant time and resources. Not understanding your message or the various needs of the wider market can also make the likelihood of succeeding on a mass level extremely challenging.

We advise starting with a solid, focused approach on a micro level. This allows for momentum. Building a local coalition of users allows for contained experimentation, leading to strategic growth. By working methodically and purposefully, you can see what elements of both your content and marketing are working, and what aren't. Eventually redoing the video and relaunching it with a larger audience down the road may have better results because of the ways you were able to tweak it when beginning small.

Next, in terms of determining an aesthetic or shooting style, every brand requires a different method and process. What will work depends upon the product and service. One brand may require documentary-style videos dictated by the sensibilities of their target audience. Another may be better reached through hilarious clips of skateboarders epically wiping out to create a sense of irreverence necessitated by a hip clientele. Either way, it comes down to research, knowing your customer.

Once again, we advise thinking like your users to appeal to them. It's important to be sure your strategy is informed by their needs, rather than what you may personally like. Taking the time to do this research will be invaluable before developing any video strategy.

Testimonial Video Secrets

Authenticity is everything. No one likes being lied to. Utilizing real people to divulge honest statements trumps fake pretenders. On top of the fact you legally must disclose actor portrayals somewhere in a video's disclaimer, it's difficult to get an actor to convincingly provide a solid testimonial.

Once you have the right person who looks good on camera, the key is to conduct an interview as if you were sitting across from them, just having coffee. You don't want to give the subject canned lines; these will prevent you from receiving good sound bites. You also don't want them to rehearse. In fact, you should probably not even offer questions ahead of time.

Posing real and authentic questions will lead to quality results. We've interviewed thousands of people, and the best moments typically occurred when going off script. Employing a director or interviewer who understands how to converse with someone in a meaningful, realistic way also helps because what looks best on videos is someone just giving authentic answers and not being told what to do. Disingenuousness is nearly impossible to mask. Most anyone watching a testimonial video can pick up a phony answer right away.

Preventing insincerity requires preemptive vetting: interviewing subjects ahead of time, asking them questions, and seeing how they fare on camera. A camera test camera can aid with this because the last thing you want is to spend considerable time and money acquiring things like a crew and a location only to discover the person is not comfortable on camera.

Mistakes like this happen all too frequently. They have happened to us. There are few things you can do to get around a bad testimonial subject. If someone isn't comfortable with lights, audio equipment, and a bunch of people watching from the beginning, it's going to be much more problematic sitting there for two to three hours just to capture a fifteen-second soundbite, which, by the way, is something we've had to do before.

Scriptwriting and Story-boarding Necessities

As discussed, every project requires an extensive pre-production process. The primary reason is to get the marketers and team members onboard, to ensure everyone knows the plan, as well as their various roles to help achieve your goals and objectives.

Having a script is always recommended, even if it's just a general outline. A storyboard is more for narrative content and visual imagery. Consisting of a series drawings, it represents the shot plans, supplying the artistic direction. Having this mapped out can do wonders when it comes to creative strategy. It will also immensely aid your director, your team, and the marketers shape the associated visuals. Most content required for small- to medium-sized businesses don't require a storyboard so much as a script and/or a shot list, as well as a capable director who knows how to put it all together.

A storyboard mostly exists so everyone in charge of the project can visually understand the story before it is shot. It also makes it easier for the people shooting the video and the talent to understand which way to move and how the camera will operate. It limits misunderstandings related to post-production.

In addition, potential questions may be avoided by consulting the storyboard. Of course, a storyboard isn't always required, but it is recommended as a general outline. A mood board can also be substituted with images, likeness, and style references. Our view is you can never plan too much so long as you understand once the camera starts rolling, things will happen beyond your control. Even so, the more preparation put into creating the video, the better the eventual payoff.

When it comes to scriptwriting as an additional means of preproduction, there are many resources to assist novices in learning the craft; however, it is important to know quality screenwriting takes time. There are many instructive great, such as *Screenplay: The*

Foundations of Screenwriting, by Syd Field, *Save the Cat: The Last Book on Screenwriting You'll Ever Need* by Blake Snyder, and *Story: Substance, Structure, Style & The Principles of Screenwriting* by Robert McKee.

These guides primarily offer instruction from a cinematic point of view, however, with an emphasis on feature-length scripts. While helpful when it comes to getting your feet wet, especially if you have never worked in this medium, they are heavy on theory, rather than practicalities. Screenwriting is an art form requiring years of experiential practice. Similar to playwriting, emphasis must be not on what's being said onscreen, but on the subtext. The very best screenwriting sets up a situation with as little words as possible, allowing the actors, their interactions, and the images onscreen to do the hard work of communicating.

Anyone who has ever tried to write a screenplay on their own will be aware of the challenge involved in learning the craft. As a society, we are used to watching endless amounts of content, from movies to TV, as well as the various videos populating YouTube. Being saturated with so much media leads many people to falsely believe screenwriting is easy. Instead, much thought and effort goes into the seemingly simplest of screen-written messages.

There is good reason why scriptwriters demand high fees. Onscreen every second counts; therefore, every word must count. Literally. What can be said with two words is far better than three. Screenwriting is a kind of language in itself, requiring technical knowledge and industry experience. It demands an understanding of production capabilities and limitations, as well insight into the ways in which humans emotionally connect through narrative.

It's important to know that though you may be the person crafting the overall vision behind your brand's message, you may not be the best person to *convey* that vision through images and words. Quickly picking up the basics of screenwriting, not to mention the subtler nuances of storytelling, is not an easy thing to accomplish. Studying is recommended, especially a close review of competitor videos, to determine their strengths and weaknesses.

Also, emulating working elements of other successful videos can be helpful to better develop your own material, rather than trying to reinvent the wheel. Still, it's important to be mindful of practical considerations.

Screenwriting's steep learning curve can be exacerbated by the significant stress involved in managing a production's logistics and costs. If you don't feel you might be the best person to deliver your message, it would be better to sub this work out to a professional because of the script's major importance. This document needs to be completed correctly, as it will be the blueprint guiding each aspect of the shoot, not to mention post-production.

Determining the Right Tone: Humor, Seriousness, a Little Bit of Both?

The importance of strategy has been a consistent theme throughout this book, and its relevance extends here. Content direction stems from strategy, which is derived from your key insights and, of course, your *Why*. It's always good to put yourself in your customer's shoes. If your target audience loves humor and reaching them in this manner wouldn't be off-putting or inappropriate in such a way that it would jeopardize your brand, you should try to create humorous videos. We say "try" because it isn't always easy to be funny onscreen.

In fact, incorporating humor can be a lot harder to do than just telling a compelling story because humor is so subjective. A single Caucasian, 21-year-old frat guy will have a way different comical barometer than a 50-year-old African American female professional with two kids. Successfully understanding your target audience may help you create a video hysterically funny for senior citizens but that most teenagers think is the dumbest thing they've ever seen. By the way, that can be totally fine if you have no intention of winning over those teens because your brand is meant for seniors.

To be certain, tone can also vary from video to video within the wider context of your overall messaging. The great thing about digital marketing is its capacity for range. Your videos needn't always follow the same format. Each video can be geared toward a different audience, and each one can project a different tone. For instance, one can be a jokey do-it-yourself spot with snarky humor. The other could be an informative thought piece.

Useful is the new cool. Useful is more important for millennials than something that's built more for entertainment's sake. A video's ability to teach you something helpful in order to better understand the world will continue to be a tried-and-true method for generating content. Educational material that leaves the viewer more knowledgeable and informed is a much better form of video marketing than just another ad preaching a product's features or the virtues of a company.

Do You Need Animated Video Content?

Animated explainer videos work well for organizations offering a complex product or service with many different service lines or products difficult to express in a single video. An animated video can be more effective in showcasing numerous scenes involving different people. Animated videos can also clarify your product's objective in ways live action cannot. Text, for instance, can be misinterpreted based on the myriad ways in which we discern what we read. Animated videos often remove the guesswork, explaining a product or service's basic functions or data in a clearer way.

Attention rates also typically scale a bit higher with animated videos than "talking-head" fare because of the more interesting, dynamic nature of the visuals. It's important to know prices vary with this medium; it's possible to find companies willing to create animated videos anywhere from $2,000 to $5,000. The price can go up from there, depending on the creative involved. Still, outsourcing animation can cost a lot less than even a single day shoot for most production companies.

Here is our rule of thumb: if your budget is low and you sell complex products, we recommend creating an animated video. If your budget is high (over $40,000) and your products are complex, it may make more sense to do some combination of an animated video and a practical shoot. Though a lot of variables come into play, an animated video may be more viable than live action as it tends to strongly resonate with audiences.

But What if You Get Stuck Creatively?

People tend to feel blocked when they don't have a good understanding of their target audience, as well as their video's main goals and objectives. One way to get around this is by sourcing inspiration. Look at competitor videos. *What is your target audience already watching? What other interesting content exists that might stir your creativity?* In order to help you combat this problem, we have included some creative exercises at videofort.com/book. If you are still feeling stuck, one of the best things to do is just start writing. It doesn't matter if it's only for ten minutes at a time. It can still get your mind working.

Applying a little competitive stress, such as deadlines, can also motivate you. Further help can come in the form of technology to this end. Flowstate, for example, is an app that punishes you if you stop writing for more than five seconds. It is based on the approach that creativity best occurs when you are in the zone of continuous production. Prior to beginning, you set how long you want to write. If you take your hands off the keyboard for more than five seconds within this time period, it will erase everything you've written. Little mental gadgets like this or restorative measures, such as exercising or meditating, can also help inspire your subconscious mind to formulate breakthrough ideas.

Personally, I won't begin developing creative or a strategy for a project unless I get at least 20 minutes of vigorous exercise or 10 minutes of quality meditation first. From there, I plug into noise-cancelling headphones with music that I've either listened to dozens of times or tracks without vocals. Everyone is different, but this practice kicks my brain into overdrive. I feel myself getting less distracted, more productive, and with better ideas on the table.

Information to Include No Matter the Video's Genre, Theme, or Tone

The content you're creating needs to be brand related. As per our discussion on content marketing, a video mustn't always be an advertisement to be commercially effective. At the same time, entertainment content isn't always the best route, either. There is much room for education and instructive fare. The goal should always guide the project, and, ultimately, the video is just one more means to sell your product or service.

Offering content tying back to your *Why* delivered in an authentic fashion will work far better than any general appeal with a quick logo slap at the end or an overt product placement. Certainly, these things can help if thoughtfully presented, but chances are someone will remember your video much better when integrated with the fundamentals of quality storytelling. We all have seen commercials we absolutely loved. They worked so well on an emotional level, yet sometimes we had no idea the name of the brand.

A great example for us was the Volkswagen commercial featuring the Darth Vader kid from the 2011 Super Bowl. It's a wonderful spot of a little boy walking through the house in his Darth Vader outfit with the John Williams' theme song playing. The story is hilarious and well-constructed. The poor kid is trying so hard to use the Force on his parents' fitness equipment, then the dog, then the dryer. Nothing seems to work. At last, he goes outside and tries extremely hard to use his powers on his dad's car. He puts his hands out, and you can really see his determination as the music builds.

The dad watches his child through the kitchen window. He starts his car with his remote-control key fob. The kid jumps up in excitement! In his mind, he's so excited because he just started the car by using the Force. Now, the Volkswagen logo was prominently displayed for a good third of the commercial, which helped with brand awareness, but it's clear the ad was not hard selling Passats. It was an interesting, funny story that got people talking.

There are thousands of great commercials like this that great stories, yet no one remembers the brand name. Yes, they may have garnered great impressions for the marketers, but they didn't necessarily build the business. This happens more frequently with bigger brands. When it comes to smaller companies, like Goldieblox, which we mentioned earlier, these often go viral because of the main message and tone. People watching the videos will most likely remember the name of the company because Goldieblox took an unconventional and important stand about preparing girls to be engineers.

Another video to go viral for similar reasons flipped the traditional conversation about young women getting their periods. Marketed by HelloFlo, this video stood out because it documented a previously invisible young girl catapulted to coolness at summer camp after receiving her "red badge" of courage. The song "Queen Bee" played over the visuals, showing how the girl became the expert to the other girls, or the "camp gyno."

In both instances, the advertised brands did it right, gaining traction and exposure through videos contextualizing their product via interesting narratives as opposed to generic product placement. Bottom line: understanding you're creating videos emphasizing your brand with elements of entertainment and information is the key to the most effective video marketing strategies and campaigns.

How to Solicit (The Right) Feedback

Once your script or video is done, you need trusted help to provide candid feedback for improvement. As your in-house team develops, having a stable of directors and producers is important to scale up. But as mentioned earlier, internal video marketing teams can get quickly overwhelmed.

Therefore, possessing the ability to sub work out to different directors or producers will provide an additional pool of resources, even if it means paying somebody a couple hundred dollars per day just to look at a script. The benefit is these individuals can provide an outsider's perspective, offering fresh insight. The more available resources and the more trusted people whose opinions you value based on their good work you have, the more you will be prepared to determine the shape, quality, and direction of your material.

Receiving unbiased critiques focused on serving the material, not personal agendas, can immensely help. A plurality of disciplines weighing in can provide even better perspective. Taking your script to the HR or sales department for a look is another great way to get an outsider's perspective from inside your organization, preventing you from having to go to someone else. It's a good idea to set up these kinds of quick meetings for review and feedback.

Beyond that, internal focus groups can be especially helpful for honest feedback. By the way, all of these suggestions are presented with the important caveat that sometimes conflicting opinion can lead to uncertainty and paralysis. Too many cooks can spoil the broth. Also, be wary of changing something you feel strongly about unless a majority of people tell you it needs modification.

Tips for Creating Engaging, Shareable Content

Good storytelling is the simplest way to connect emotionally. This motif is a recurring theme within the book because its importance cannot be overstated. The principal elements of narrative matter: the background or context, character establishment, and plot development. These are vital in order to emotionally connect with an audience.

IKEA had an amazing commercial back in the early 2000's based on a lamp. The lamp was the main character, and it sat on the desk. The owner loved the lamp. He would go turn it on, work all night, and turn it off. The way they shot the commercial created a persona behind the lamp, as if it was a real character. It looked happy, just shining light. Just as quickly as the commercial began, time went by and the lamp became old and dated. The owner placed it out on the street during a stormy night.

Sad music played as rain poured down on the lamp. The camera looked up at the window where a new lamp sat, emanating light with the old lamp silhouetted, looking up at the building. As a viewer, you began to feel empathy for the lamp, ignoring the fact that this lamp is just an inanimate object. Suddenly, a Swedish man in a large trench coat stepped into the frame, staring directly into the camera, "Why do you care about this lamp?" he asked. "It has no feelings. It's just a lamp. The new one is better!" He then exited frame and an IKEA Call to action ended the commercial.

What's amazing about this story is how the little lamp made the viewers invest in its well-being through imagery and sound. Then, suddenly reality smacked you in the face with the Swedish man's interjection. The clever storytelling delivered such an unexpected emotional impact, it's still discussed by my marketing colleagues to this day.

Audiences connected with the material, shared it, engaged with it. Like any good art, it led to contentious discussions. Some people sided with the IKEA man; others still felt bad for the lamp, in spite of his words. Of course, it's brilliant for another reason. IKEA sells lamps. It's all about home furnishings that must be bought and replaced for the company to stay profitable. This spot was the perfect, cheeky way for them to say, "You need to buy even more stuff from us." The takeaway here is to embrace story when expressing your message. It's the best way to make a powerful, lasting impression.

Now that we have set the stage, illuminating the many facets of production and content, let's make the conversation about you. The next chapter will discuss ways to revolutionize your business with video advertising.

CHAPTER TEN: Revolutionize Your Business with Video Advertising

"Early to bed, early to rise, work like hell, and advertise."
– Ted Turner, Media Mogul

Undercover Tourist: Shortcutting Awareness through Video Content

Undercover Tourist is an authorized supplier of online discount tickets to such popular attractions as Disney World, Universal Studios, and SeaWorld. It helps tourists save money and avoid waiting in long lines. Ian Ford, the company founder and CEO, stumbled onto the concept of video advertising by accident. He was trying to explain his company's business to his young son. When Mr. Ford realized simply explaining the business model wasn't getting through, he decided to use video as a better means of explanation.

This epiphany led Ford to post videos on YouTube that contained travel tips and timesaving advice for adults, as well as a series about attractions and activities for kids. According to Ford, "Our formula on YouTube video is simple and effective. We shoot authentic, point-of-view, unslick content with a steady hand and slow pans. We engage people with the experience itself rather than overwhelm them with a corporate voice." He nailed one of the key aspects of successful video campaigns: allowing room for an emotional connection to the experience always makes a video more memorable.

Taking full advantage of YouTube's power and popularity as a search engine, Undercover Tourist used video not to sell tickets, but for content marketing. He created a rich array of free and actionable tips on how to navigate a family adventure. Soon enough, Ford was able to utilize his YouTube channel to promote the business itself—sending viewers to his website for further info on basics, like nearby hotels and easy car rentals.

The site also included an accessible blog with insight on where to find healthy snacks, how to meet character celebrities, and how to get free souvenirs. The result of this content combination is that Undercover Tourist's family-friendly videos, backed by solid and actionable information, established the brand as a trusted travel advisor.

The company's YouTube channel accumulated over 46k subscribers and surpassed 38 million video views during its first 5 years. On average, that's over 600k video views per month, or close to 20k every single day. With every video linking back to UndercoverTourist.com, the resulting traffic was phenomenal for an initiative begun as an experiment.

The Attention Battle: YouTube vs Facebook

As Undercover Tourist learned, the world of advertising is changing. Traditional advertising methods, like print and television, are being replaced by video advertising at an astounding rate. Moreover, Facebook and Instagram are taking video market share, by way of attention, away from YouTube. This growth rate is faster than any other medium, excluding mobile, and much faster than traditional online display advertising, which has slowed to three percent annually. How-

ever, the real question is what platform is best: You-
Tube or Facebook?

YouTube is the largest web provider of video content delivery with over one billion unique visits each
month. It's the second largest search engine in the
world, and the amount of content uploaded daily is
mind boggling. Now, if we take a deeper look at this
platform, the two most popular video types are Product
Review Videos and How-To Videos, followed by Vlogs
(Video Blog), Gaming Videos & Comedy/Skit videos.
The behavioral trait displayed by consumers utilizing
YouTube is discovery. Users are seeking information
and answers, similar to how people use Google's search
engine. Additionally, most users seek entertainment
when engaging with the platform. It's rare for people
to browse YouTube without any preconceived notions
about the content they want to consume.

Facebook, on the other hand, was built to garner
attention and keep you captivated with as little effort
as possible. Users' behavior tends to be more passive.
They tend to scroll through their feed, only pausing for
content they find interesting. Even more interesting-
ly, according to wordstream.com, 85 percent of videos
viewed on Facebook are watched without sound.

Importantly, both platforms possess a pay-to-play
model when it comes to organic audience exposure. If
you want people to see your content, you need to place
media dollars behind it, even if you have a pre-existing following. Additionally, YouTube videos posted on
Facebook receive 10x less engagement than the same
video natively posted on Facebook, according to So-
cialbakers.com. This makes sense when considering
these companies' competing nature. Everyone, and I
mean everyone, is trying to garner attention—to keep

users on their site for as long as possible. If 50 percent of users who watch a YouTube video on Facebook happen to click on the YouTube link (as opposed to watching it in their feed), 50 percent of Facebook's users will have left the platform. To avoid this situation, Facebook has built-in tools, such as auto-play and auto-captions, to make the user experience as simple and easy as possible.

Yet the question remains: which platform is better for you and your brand? The answer: both. There's one caveat, however. The content you post needs to be custom-tailored for each specific platform. Remember, YouTubers actively search for specific content. Thus, the posted content should include a summary of what will occur throughout the rest of the video. Yes, you may have more time to engage with your audience than on Facebook, but we're still talking about seconds here, not minutes. For Facebook, you have even less time to get your audience's passive attention.

Hollywood has caught on to these viewing behaviors. In particular, movie studios use a fundamentally different approach to launching their trailers. Many promotional trailers now broadcast brief ads (up to five seconds) for themselves on Facebook before the trailer. However, on YouTube, trailers are created and posted in their standard format. The idea for posting differently on Facebook is that they want to let users know what they're about to watch is going to be awesome. This strategy is worth taking into consideration for your own branded content.

Ultimately, posting natively to both platforms can offer your content the greatest opportunity for maximum exposure. When creating evergreen content, it's worth noting that "how-to" videos are better suited for

YouTube. On YouTube, audiences are more inclined to search for your content. In comparison, on Facebook, only limited audiences will stop and watch instructions on how to install a garage door. Recognizing this reality and knowing how users on Facebook are looking to connect with people, catch up on news, and be entertained, you can post a Facebook-specific video, highlighting your coolest garage door installations. By doing so, you will be in a better position to capture a wider audience with entertaining and passive entertainment best suited for Facebook.

Ultimately, online video continues to present amazing opportunities television and print media simply cannot. Not only that, it's accessible on hundreds of millions of mobile devices globally. YouTube patrons represent a hyper-engaged, highly-connected, younger audience. For your business, this translates to tremendous potential. Brian Halligan, founder of HubSpot Inc., was quoted on the New York Stock Exchange website shortly after his company's stock went public. He said, "The Internet has created an entirely new, empowered consumer, and there's no fooling them. Everything is being Yelpified." Halligan was referring to the way crowd-sourced information has become critical for business, demanding a certain base level of transparency. What's also interesting to note is his company's strategy was influenced by the Grateful Dead's model. HubSpot owes its success to giving away quality content.

There are numerous ways to use video to promote your business. Whichever method you ultimately use, you want to ensure it will be noticed and that it will be better than the competition's offering. The key to making the jump from good to great is having a strong, well-conceived strategy. That may sound self-evident, but surprisingly, only 44 percent of B2B marketers have a strategy in place. The following steps will help your business define and develop an optimal content strategy using video.

Build Your Video Marketing Strategy

Step one: identify your audience

For any business, understanding who your customers and potential customers are is the key to developing a marketing strategy. Even small businesses can use public information sources to learn more about their target audiences.

Online sources like census.gov and the Bureau of Labor statistics have data free for the taking. Owned marketing properties like websites and ad campaigns can also reveal demographic information about user interests through user-submitted data. Any remaining holes can be filled in through independent market research, including online surveys and focus groups.

A market research survey is another effective way to gauge customer satisfaction and/or test the waters for a new product or service. Surveys can also provide insight about customer buying habits, brand awareness, and market size. Most important, they fill in the blanks as to what drives your consumers and why your strategies may or may not resonate with them. Focus groups, on the other hand, are more about gathering opinions from a select, live audience. The participants watch a presentation or interact with a physical product, then give their personal impressions in a generally informal setting while their responses are evaluated.

All of these tools can help you better understand your audience, what they have versus what they want or need, and how you can fill that gap. Look for patterns and trends, such as the average salary for first-time home buyers, education level, where they live, what they buy—put yourself in your customers' mindset.

Business-to-business branding (B2B) refers to commerce transactions between businesses, such as between a manufacturer and a wholesaler, or between a wholesaler and a retailer. For businesses in the B2B space, content marketing can mean solving customers' biggest problems, anticipating their future needs, and becoming the go-to for those solutions.

For example, the software company, Adobe, recognized its central graphics applications were receiving strong competition from numerous free or inexpensive options on the market. Grappling with this new competition, Adobe restructured its core business model. After taking a close look at its customers' most serious graphics-related problems, Adobe devised a solution. The result was the Marketing Cloud, a new platform aiding web retailers to ensure all websites show the correct images to customers, while also offering analytics and campaign management tools to help businesses grow.

Through content marketing, Adobe promoted this new product by engaging over 20 experts to create blog posts and deliver speeches at digital-marketing forums worldwide. These individuals provided key insights to e-commerce companies, solving their problems and in the process, promoting the new platform Adobe had developed. And Adobe's efforts paid off—the Marketing Cloud is now their biggest source of revenue.

Business-to-customer (B2C) businesses aren't missing out on the content marketing revolution, either. In 2014, 90 percent of B2C marketers were using content marketing, with 60 percent planning to increase the amount of resources allocated to this endeavor.

Step two: audit your brand position

Once you understand who your audience is, the next step is to determine where you are positioned in the current marketplace. Information about your brand position is not always available at your fingertips. Customer reviews typically provide incomplete and skewed data about how your brand is performing.

To get the needed information, you'll have to do your own research. A marketing survey is a good place to start: collect data on market share and delve into how customers feel about your brand in relation to its competitors. Again, focus groups can also provide insight from a limited group for more immediate feedback. Google Surveys is a simple and easy solution if you don't have any experience creating your own survey. Go to https://www.google.com/analytics/surveys/ for more information.

Next, look at your own site traffic and social media channels, then track any trends you can detect. Pay attention to other social media apps, from Yelp to Facebook, and conduct a blog search for mentions of your company or product offerings. Put yourself in your customers' shoes and keep asking, "How do people feel about our brand on a day-to-day basis, and how do they weigh us against the competition?" Once you have a bead on this, you will be in a better position to shape a content strategy responding to your customer needs in context of the market.

Step three: set goals

Now that you know where your company stands, you can begin to develop a realistic plan about where you want to be and how you to get there.

Use the below SMART model to guide your goal-setting activities. This matrix will keep you accountable and working within realistic guidelines.

SMART goals are:

Specific — pertaining to a particular context or metric

Measurable — comparable using concrete numbers

Attainable — challenging, but doable given your current resources

Relevant — offering direct value in the context of your current situation

Time-sensitive — bound to a deadline

Step four: define your unique value proposition

As we know, there's a lot of content out there—but there's also a lot of redundancy. Determine what you can offer that's unique. Determine what sets you apart from all the other noisemakers. It can be difficult to pin down, but doing the hard work now to define your unique value proposition will allow you to develop and compete long term. Be careful to not just list unique features and benefits. Instead, your unique value proposition should focus on your *Why*, which we discussed previously.

Step five: develop a clear style guideline

Once you know your content direction, it's time to focus on delivery. This is a branding personality issue as much as anything else. Your brand needs to present a consistent look and voice to the world or your efforts at differentiation will be lost. Engaging experts is worthwhile to help you develop a set of style guidelines to express your brand voice and visual identity clearly and consistently.

As you develop your video marketing strategy, keep in mind the following lessons culled from content marketing experts:

Being authentic means being in touch with your audience.

At its core, content marketing works because it allows your business and your customers to develop a more engaging relationship.

It is better to keep it simple than to go over your audience's heads.

Your business possesses a great deal of specialized knowledge. Make sure your communications are relevant and accessible to your target customers.

Media channels are marketing channels.

Never forget your media channels must be giving customers what they want—or they will go elsewhere to get it.

It's not enough to just have great information.

The information presented should be valuable and relevant to your customers.

Know yourself, know your audience—and the rest will come.

Great content and genuine interaction come from a combination of self-knowledge and audience knowledge.

Subtlety matters, even if no one notices.

Use language your audience can understand, but throw in a relatable story or factual statistics for powerful reinforcement. Keep examples relevant to provide explicit clarification and validity of your point.

Wherever inspiration is found, go there.

Follow your muse.

Workplace culture is an asset.

With a strong internal culture, your day-to-day interactions and personality can inform your content, presenting popular ideas in a unique way to enhance readers' experience and to make your content stand out from the crowd.

Be a hub, not a megaphone.

Create videos encouraging video responses to further the conversation. Use your marketing channels as a place to spark dialogue, to gauge the needs of your customers, and mine future ideas. Above all, make something meaningful and enriching.

Marketing is a relationship.

Marketing should be a two-way street, making businesses appear confident and customers feel appreciated.

Never expect customers to come to you.

Wherever the buyers are, businesses must meet them and create content interesting them, enriching them. This will entice the customer to want more.

The old tactics don't work as well as they used to.

With the capacity for engagement and discussion opening new avenues for businesses, methods that do not facilitate this kind of activity simply no longer meet consumer expectations.

Curation may be just as valuable as creation (though not a substitute).

Content marketing in its purest form is about delivering value to your customers, whether this comes from your business or another.

Success lies where your knowledge and your audience's interests meet.

Information falls into two distinct categories:
1. What you know
2. What your audience wants to know.

Success falls at the intersection between the two.

Stop soliciting, start providing.

Marketing relationships and human relationships are virtually one and the same. The two abide by one common rule: Great relationships are predicated on giving and sharing, not asking and taking.

Great content inspires action.

This action can come in many forms, but the key barometer of "great" content is whether or not it inspires viewers to do something.

Great content is also irreplaceable.

There's a lot of noise out there. Make sure your content does not just duplicate other available information, but rather presents it in a unique and unforgettable way.

Consistency is not just important, it's a necessity.

Consistency builds trust, reliability, and accountability.

Content marketing is part of a larger marketing plan.

Content marketing is only one part of a larger marketing effort—be careful not to mistake the tool for the task.

Pass the Logo Test

Every piece of video content you create should noticeably resemble your brand. The look and feel must remain consistent not only throughout your campaign, but between different mediums, like your website, print collateral, and the like. Simply put, you should be able to answer the following question with an outstanding NO: If I were to put a competitor's logo at the end of this video, would the video still work?

ShoppersChoice: A YouTube Success Story Ripe for Emulation

When ShoppersChoice began in 1998, it was just a small mom-and-pop store selling barbecues in Baton Rouge, Louisiana. Today, the company is one of the leading online resources for grills, outdoor furniture, and accessories, having more than doubled its workforce. The company pulled off this transformation through YouTube videos. ShoppersChoice used its YouTube channel, BBQGuys, to offer consumers an immersive experience into the barbecue industry. Not only did product demos introduce viewers to the latest equipment, but ShoppersChoice's own chef, Tony Matassa, shared his favorite recipes and tips for at-home grilling.

ShoppersChoice continues to take full advantage of YouTube's True View features to run campaigns, find quality leads, and drive traffic to their website. In fact, whenever ShoppersChoice adds new content to its channel, it observes spikes in traffic to its site. With help from True View, their daily views jumped from 800 to 900 to around 5,300. The cost for this exponential increase in traffic is a mere $3 to $5 per day budget, at 2 to 3 cents per click, proving that with the right content, even small companies can use online video advertising to transform their business.

Now that we know video works and the steps needed to revolutionize your business online through strategic content, let's explore more innovative marketing strategies to grow your brand.

CHAPTER ELEVEN: Video Types & Tactics

"The aim of marketing is to know and understand the customer so well the product or service fits him and sells itself."

~Peter Drucker, Educator

It's essential to determine the best type of video, or tactic, to convey your chosen message for maximum promotional impact. Your video's purpose will set the style choice, whether promoting a new brand, educating existing customers, or informing about social outreach. No matter the myriad number of uses, there is a specific way each video can be produced to optimally target the appropriate audience and meet its intended goal.

The following video styles and tactics possess a unique purpose and advantage. Each will be easily recognizable. They can be repeatedly seen throughout YouTube and across the Internet because they work. In fact, we are so used to seeing them we probably do not even notice when watching television or online videos.

For instance, in many cases, the simple choice of a "talking head" or a well-framed interview can automatically bestow the viewer with the unconscious recognition they are watching authoritative content. One final note, as we will discuss more thoroughly at the end of this chapter, storytelling is still the key to any video's success. Marketing in any medium continually works best with good narrative.

Talking Head

Talking head videos are the basic platform of conveying a direct message. It's best to position the speaker directly in front of the camera, looking into the lens and speaking to the audience.

The traditional version is framed in a medium or close-up shot. Done correctly, this style offers a personal touch to directly connect with the viewer. The use of an authoritative performance also provides a kind of teacher/student dynamic. With the right affable talent, it may even simulate the experience of being in the same room and learning from a friend.

Interview

A variation on the talking head video, the interview style generally focuses on multiple people in a question-and-answer format. One person is either the interviewer or moderator; the other featured person (or multiple people) will either be a professional "expert" or have practical experience with the video's subject. Interview videos also have the advantage of being authoritative without seeming too preachy as the spokesperson is replaced by a surrogate for the audience.

Generally, the interviewer or moderator is inquisitive, just as the viewer is, thereby encouraging the audience to be more open to the information provided by the expert(s). Ultimately, the knowledge is on display, not so much the expert, which can greatly highlight the value of a product, service, or program.

Over the years, I've prided myself on being a great interviewer—not because I can read questions eloquently, but because I'm always looking for ways to get the subject to forget there are cameras in the room. If you've ever been interviewed on camera or witnessed an interview, you probably know people tend to freak out when cameras start rolling. Otherwise confident speakers turn into babbling buffoons. I've seen it hundreds of times.

Avoid this predicament by starting with softball questions. Warm your subjects up a bit. *What's your name? Where are you from? What did you think of the (insert topical event)?* The key here is to get your subject's body to absorb their pumping adrenaline and calm down, which typically can take between two to four minutes. Once your subject is more at ease, you can begin asking more challenging questions. However, I rarely stick to the exact script. I always listen to my subject's answers and frequently ask them to elaborate or hit on key points. It's important to frame the interview as if you and the subject are just out having coffee. The best interviews are those where the subject feels comfortable diving deep into their answers.

Slide Show Presentations

Not everyone loves PowerPoint, but there is no denying slides with a good voiceover narration are often a simple, clear way to convey ideas or data. When the message is straightforward, relying on graphics to tell the most compelling story—whether it be pie charts, data graphs, or documentary photographs— sometimes a slide show is the best method to use.

While most suited toward data-driven messages, slide shows can also be infused with humor or an emotional punch. Additionally, they are often easy to produce when resources do not allow for on-screen talent or location shooting.

Webinars

Utilizing a combination of techniques, webinars are essentially recorded presentations designed to teach the viewer something. Similar to a lecture, they can combine helpful graphics and edited video or animation. Some webinars are built upon slide show presentations. Often, the presenter is simply a talking head; other times, there may be a "live" audience, or multiple presenters However, the emphasis is generally on educating the viewer regarding a specific topic.

Animated Video

As mentioned in chapter eight, animation has become increasingly affordable and no longer the exclusive domain of studios with deep pockets. Flash animation revolutionized web video in the 1990s, but there are many options today for generating quality animation suitable for presentations without any programming or art skills required.

Various websites and apps can provide different animation types at little cost. These won't necessarily look like they were produced by Pixar, but they can allow for a greater range of creative flexibility while planning the next sales pitch or demonstration.

Photo Montage

A form of slide show presentation, a photo montage is simply a collection of still images. Generally accompanied by music or narration, a good photo montage tells a story or develops a visual theme.

In the wake of 9/11 and the destruction of the Twin Towers in New York City, there were many photo montages of the first responders that went viral. The patriotic theme and inspirational storyline was clearly conveyed in the often-brilliant still images captured during the hectic day. Employing a simple musical background, the photo montages were powerful messages that rallied people together, helped heal wounds, and otherwise presented a horrific event in a profound light.

Animal rights activists have similarly used photo montages to show cute images of different species playing together or helping one another, especially when one species is a natural predator. Gun control advocates have also utilized this technique to highlight images of families after mass shootings.

Documentary film producer Ken Burns has made a career of feature-length photo montages covering historical events, including the television mini-series, *The Civil War*. In fact, the editing technique of zooming and panning across a photograph was labeled the "Ken Burns Effect," in the first version of Apple's iMovie software. It allowed for a quick and easy assembly of digital stills into video format with only a few mouse clicks.

Sales Pitch

Typically used on a product landing page, the sales pitch is often found right above a click-to-buy button or a link to "opt-in" to a service. The sales pitch video may appear as the only content on the page, or it may be accompanied by a written pitch and testimonials.

Marketing studies have shown potential customers are often more likely to watch a video than they are to read the entirety of a transcript. Additionally, a sales pitch video has the benefit of being able to both show and tell at the same time, encouraging either

an impulse buy or making the case for a serious purchase.

Launch Series

A collection of videos leading up to a product launch,
these are generally part of a larger sales pitch. The series may consist of several educational videos designed
to drive anticipation, while also providing useful content. Importantly, these videos offer a way to quickly
establish credibility before making a direct sales pitch
that is the culmination of the series.

Testimonials

As previously discussed, the testimonial is excellent
for generating credibility (when done correctly). The
Internet is overflowing with reviews and commentary
on just about everything, but concerns about the authenticity of online reviews can make their value ques-
tionable. Often, written testimonials, though useful,
can be seen as too anonymous to be taken seriously.

A video testimonial, on the other hand, has the
power of authenticity behind it; the viewer sees the
person making the endorsement, thus fostering a personal bond with the viewer. Not only is the testimonial
a handy tool for recording customer or client feedback
on their experiences with a product or service, it can
also bolster brand recognition and company credibility
at the same time. In fact, many potential customers or
clients tend to value the information from a testimonial video more highly than they would from a sales
pitch or talking head.

Packaged Video

Sometimes the video itself is the product, packaged for
sale via download or occasionally as a DVD or Blue-

Ray disk. The types of videos sold this way are informative in nature, often recordings of webinars or lectures. These items may be tied directly to a launch series and sales pitch, all of which may offer a solid introduction to the paid video.

If the subject of the product video is well established or the content is presented by a well-known individual, it may also sell well on its own or require only a good testimonial to market it appropriately. Ultimately, however, these packaged videos are still sales tools in their own right. Because the consumer is buying them, there is weighted credibility for the brand. These videos may also utilize or reference items or services in a way that promotes more than mere brand awareness.

Live Webcasts

The increasingly popular—and increasingly easy to produce—live webcast allows events to be shared in real time and archived for later. The element of timeliness can exploit an existing market or user base while raising anticipation levels.

The sense of immediacy involved in a live streaming event adds both urgency and intimacy to the experience. The audience becomes a participant, actively involved in keeping up with the proceedings.

Of all the styles of web video, the live webcast demands the greatest level of connectedness from the viewer, beginning with the commitment to join at the specified time. However, the ability to archive these webcasts for later viewing adds a layer for both the original viewers and those who missed it the first time around.

Depending on the available equipment and re-sources, the webcast can have the look and feel of a live television event complete with multiple cameras, or it can be streamed entirely from a single mobile phone using a range of inexpensive (or even free) apps.

No longer must a live streaming video originate from behind an office desk and look choppy and pixi-lated as it sputters through the Internet. With a high-speed data connection and a hi-def webcam, there are few hindrances determining when and where a live webcast may be shot and how great it can look.

Live Demos

A subset of the live webcast, a live demo specifically focuses on product or service engagement in real time. Beyond a typical webcast, however, a live demo often incorporates or combines a slide show presentation with a talking head-style video. Frequently used to simulate a teaching experience, the live demo may also require a more sophisticated technological foundation if it is meant to combine media elements; however, it can also be as simple as a table-top demonstration.

Recorded Demos or Screencasts

Using a similar approach to the live demo, a recorded demo allows for more flexibility as to how the video is constructed. Combining various elements as neces-sary, a recorded demo can be a fully mixed-media ex-perience. This style also frees up creativity with regard to where it is shot, the type of equipment used and more. And, of course, there are those locations where a live video simply would not be a practical option or where multiple takes might be required to get the shot just right.

On the flipside of this is the screencast. When all of the necessary information for the video is on the computer screen, making a recording of the screen image (with the possible addition of narration) may be the perfect solution. Screencasts can be done live but are usually recorded to demonstrate a process that can be easily reviewed.

Photo-retouching or software tutorials are examples in which a screencast may be the best stylistic choice. Screencasts can also capture cursor movement and any video or audio played on the computer. In essence, whatever the person making the video sees, that is what is recorded. The subsequent file can usually be edited and combined with any other video material.

Video Emails

Utilizing existing resources is always a good way to begin, and one often underused resource available to many business owners is their email list. A website is a terrific tool for building an email list of interested current and potential clients or customers. Connecting with these individuals is often best accomplished through a video email.

By connecting directly with a select group that has opted in to receive these video communications, a brand can easily strengthen its core message and offer exclusive content or encourage early adopting of new offerings.

Most video emails are embedded rather than attached, meaning they do not slow down an email connection or require the viewer to store them on a computer or mobile device.

By utilizing an embed code in the email message, the video can actually stream straight from YouTube or a similar service while appearing to play directly within the email message, like a traditional newsletter, combined with rich media content.

Video Tip Series

This is a very popular promotional tool, especially with dedicated YouTube channels. As we know, YouTube is an easy and virtually ubiquitous platform for establishing a strong media presence. Creating a channel dedicated to offering tips related to your product or business is a powerful way to stake out a leadership position in any field. These videos can also help improve a site's overall SEO (search engine optimization), especially with new search algorithms favoring media-rich websites.

Know Your Purpose

Beyond the styles of video that can be produced, there are also specific reasons to consider why a video should be created. By understanding the purpose, the style can be better determined. Video is especially good for explaining concepts or ideas. It is also far more efficient than text at displaying problems and their solutions or explaining processes taking place over time and a wide distance. A good script accompanied by effective visuals can make complex ideas easier to understand and more fun to explore.

Introduction Videos

The introduction video is helpful for entrepreneurs and sole proprietors whose businesses depend on personal relationships and trust. It offers a business the opportunity to address potential clients and customers directly. Personality, areas of expertise, and relevant credentials are easy to display. This is also an ideal pathway to begin building relationships that will be key to the brand's success.

Real estate professionals, personal physicians, and business advisors of all stripes may benefit from a good introduction video. Done right, such content will attract new clients or help engage existing customers with a business trying to increase brand awareness.

Product Video

The ever-popular product video is usually a 30- to 90-second spot, much like a television commercial, with the focus on the product and what it can do. Such videos tend to avoid minutia, concentrating instead on the high-level benefits afforded to the consumer. A product video can be live action or animated, depending on the product and the personality of the brand.

Tour Videos

While they may appear to be the domain of travel services, the tour video has much broader potential applications. Any business providing services rather than products can utilize video to generate a virtual tour of what the business offers, bringing viewers a visual experience akin to a personal visit.

Certainly, hotels, resorts, and cruise ships can make good use of a tour video, but so can restaurants and convention facilities, circuses, or hospitals. Any business can show off its properties, bringing its particular experience to the viewer, thereby creating welcoming intimacy with potential clients.

Lifestyle Videos

Popular with travel businesses and real estate professionals, the lifestyle video is being used more frequently by retailers, as well. In-store displays or kiosks run videos showcasing products appealing to the aspirations of the customers.

The Go-Pro video camera, which easily attaches to any sort of helmet or vehicle, has been heavily branded through in-store lifestyle videos presenting first-person views of extreme sports. Monitors displaying POV footage of skiing, skateboarding, dirt bike racing, or parachuting can drive product sales in stores where customers go for outdoor apparel designed for these sports.

Though a surf shop is not the first place one would look for a new video camera, the Go-Pro can sell itself by aligning with the lifestyle and aspirational nature of the surf shop's client base.

Product Demo

In addition to the overview provided in a standard product video, the product demo shows the consumer how the product works. The nature of the product will help determine the style of the video; live action employee demonstrations work well for some products, while screencasts typically work best for software or other digital products. Animation often enhances videos for medical devices or technical equipment—especially when the "action" takes place inside a difficult to observe area, whether it be the human body, a computer motherboard, or an internal combustion engine.

How-to-Videos

How-to-videos demonstrate exactly how to set up, use a product, or complete a task. These D.I.Y. instructional videos are often used by large corporations, like The Home Depot, which has a YouTube channel devoted to lessons on a wide range of building and renovation tasks for do-it-yourselfers.

For many customers, the how-to video is much easier to understand than text-only instructions. Offering a how-to video that a customer genuinely needs can create a sense of connection and engagement impossible to similarly foster through just the printed word. And with easy-to-follow instructions, these videos can create the added benefit of customer gratitude.

Thought Leadership

Some videos are not designed to sell anything directly, but rather focus on establishing brand credibility or company awareness. Businesses have been using this type of content for a long time in many ways. Law firms produce newsletters with articles about legislation or important rulings; industry magazines publish articles about current trends or systemic problems.

Providing customers with useful information while establishing expertise and trust is the goal of thought leadership videos. Having a library of such content can be a particularly valuable asset.

Storytelling is Essential

As mentioned throughout this book, successful marketing revolves around narrative. Marketer Neil Patel continually points out on his eponymous blog how good storytelling can sell products in any medium. He cites the 1982 example of Hasbro's collaboration with Marvel comics to bring the G.I. Joe character to the page, hoping to replicate some of the merchandising lightning that Marvel helped Kenner Toys exploit with its line of Star Wars action figures.

This partnership worked crazy well, with sales of G.I. Joe toys increasing dramatically in the wake of the new comic. In addition, the marketing aspect aided Marvel, too. The publisher saw the new G.I. Joe title become one of its top sellers within seven years of launch.

The bulk of this chapter was a thorough examination of the numerous and varied content marketing techniques video provides. It is our hope that by sharing the myriad possibilities for material, it spurred creative thinking within you as to what may be your most viable approach. As we have consistently seen, in today's market, the best place for content marketing is online.

Meanwhile, the most expressive, easily digestible medium for consumers is online video. Telling stories, using the styles discussed here as starting points to craft your message and build your brand, is what video was designed for. Understanding the basic styles, as well as their purposes, is an important step toward defining a company's branding strategy.

The (Not-So) Secret Ingredient: One More Word about Story

Storytelling is the hardest simple thing to do. The difference between a good and a great story relates to a myriad of different elements coming together in the most complete form. It requires talent, understanding, and finesse. The phrase, "Content is king," has been around for a while, reflecting the reality that a good story is what keeps people coming back. Quality content offers something more than what is expected, whether in terms of useful, actionable information or simply entertainment value. And the best content is conveyed through tales with a beginning, middle, and end.

According to the consulting firm, PQ Media, roughly $145 billion was spent on content marketing in 2014, signaling this concept has clearly been embraced by the mainstream. But dollars invested in content do not immediately translate to a good R.O.I. unless the material itself is developed in such a way it resonates with audiences.

In his article, *Become a Binge-Worthy Brand*, Tom Gerace perfectly summarizes this need: "There is a storytelling craft—like there is with any art—that lies behind those stories that connect with us, make us feel happy/sad/anxious/angry, and cause us to lose ourselves in the tale being told. Studies show when these specific story elements weave together—the characters, setting, and rising conflict—our minds react almost as if we are experiencing the events in the story ourselves. Smart marketers know that the emotions stories elicit are powerful things, and brands that tell great stories can build strong connections with their customers through them."

One of the studies Gerace refers to is the work done by Berkeley University's Paul Zak. The research done in Zak's lab is focused on why the brain loves stories, what makes stories effective, and how stories "bring brains together." This last idea is so paramount, as it shows the neural mechanism of emotional stimulation is the basis for how humans form relationships based on large-scale cooperation and empathy.

The neurochemical oxytocin has been identified as being responsible for empathy, as well as narrative transportation. Zak's studies have shown that as oxytocin is synthesized, the effect is to make people more trustworthy, generous, and compassionate. While Zak's work also reinforces the common wisdom that people learn better through stories, it is not the case that every video or story is effective. One of the primary takeaways from these experiments at Berkeley is that a solid understanding of the "dramatic arc" matters.

Whether it is called "the hero's journey" or "universal story structure," one thing is clear: a dramatic arc (including a crisis and a climax) clicks something in the brain that makes a story—and its lessons—stick with the viewer. This is true even if part of the story, or elements of the narrative arc, are simply implied. Not surprisingly, Zak also reported that, building on the notion that "the medium is the message," video connects neurologically in a stronger manner than text. This strong sense of empathic transportation is a key element as to why video is such a good medium for storytelling and why it is essential for all content developers to understand this unique skill.

Here are a couple of fantastic books that will help you become a better storyteller: The Storytelling Animal: How Stories Make Us Human by Jonathan Gottschall, The Story Factor: Inspiration, Influence, and Persuasion through the Art of Storytelling, by Annette Simmons and Doug Lipman, and Resonate: Present Visual Stories that Transform Audiences by Nancy Duarte.

Now that we more fully understand the various types of video, as well as the necessities of good storytelling, it is time to take your brand to the next level by determining the best distribution plan.

CHAPTER TWELVE: Video Distribution

"Content is king, but distribution is queen ... and she wears the pants."

-Jonah Peretti, CEO of Buzzfeed

But First, Some Helpful Terminology

The new media landscape continues to evolve so quickly it is often difficult to keep up with emerging lexicon. Even when terms have been around for a few years, it can be tricky to get a handle on what everything means and when it applies. Before diving into the ins and outs of digital video distribution and interactive marketing, let's simplify the discussion by defining a few key terms integral to the business.

Owned Media

Refers to an advertising channel owned by a website or a blog. For example, a company's Facebook page and Twitter account are co-owned with their respective hosts. A company's blog on its own site is also wholly owned by that company.

Paid Media

Paid media refers to advertising a brand pays for. It may include things like display ads, television spots, sponsorships, paid search results, and Internet display ads. This is rooted in the old media model of advertising—buying ad space—but is still very relevant to modern websites.

Earned Media

Earned media refers to a situation in which customers spread your message for you through word of mouth, often via sharing on social media sites or viral video. This is the most effective way to advertise because the customer drives the message's dissemination. Not only are they doing it for free, it is out of desire to share good content. The media is "earned" by being well made, informative, entertaining, and/or worthwhile. This is the crux of content marketing and, in some ways, the Holy Grail of advertising.

The Owned, Paid and Earned Media Models in Effect

All three of these terms have an important role in a well-planned advertising mix. Taken together, they provide a simple matrix to categorize and prioritize the media choices being made for your brand. Let's look at ways some of these categories could be put to effective use by examining a few hypothetical (and not-so-hypothetical) scenarios.

The Super Bowl continues to draw attention for the television commercials aired during the game. It is one of the few television events in which many viewers make it a point to stay tuned during the commercial breaks, often debating which spots worked best. If a major national corporation, like Home Depot, chooses to advertise during the Super Bowl, the first step toward airing their spot is buying air time from the network showing the game. If Home Depot wants the commercial to run multiple times during the game, additional air time must be purchased for each instance.

This is typical for paid media. The rules say that if a company wants its commercial to run, it must pay for media space. The same is true for print advertising on a billboard, whether it be in Times Square or along a dusty stretch of Route 66. Similarly, Coca-Cola could commission a movie about its storied history and then purchase a block of basic cable airtime during which to run the program.

Paying for media space and time is an effective way to reach a captive audience in the right place at the right time to receive the message. There are, of course, innumerable outlets for this type of media, limited only by available advertising real estate. Basically, wherever there is a blank wall at a sporting event, a free video monitor in a convention hall, available billboard space along a highway, magazine pages, television and radio time, inserts with purchased goods—anywhere it's possible to spread a message—there will be opportunity for a brand to capitalize on the paid media model.

In today's interactive world where digital messaging is the driving format, mixing the best of print and video, websites are eager to sell space for paid media-rich advertising. Stalwarts, like Google AdWords, offer a multitude of plans for every budget. Paid media is, quite literally, everywhere in both the physical and virtual worlds we inhabit.

Earned media requires a place to be experienced, much like paid media does, in an environment where the audience will be inclined to look. The biggest difference, however, is that earned media comes presented by a trusted third party: a friend, business, or entertainment outlet, because of its unique nature and value.

Red Bull exemplified this strategy with the brand's now famous space jump. By strapping a camera to a helmet and recording the real-time parachuting experience of the highest jump on record, one man's feat became more than an advertising stunt: it became news. Initially intended to appeal to extreme sports aficionados, a prime target demographic for Red Bull's energy drinks, this stunt transcended the perceived audience and became the topic of conversation around water coolers worldwide.

Red Bull pulled off something so audacious it earned the right for its brand to be talked about as well as shared, repeatedly, through private messages, social media, blogs of all stripes, and numerous news and entertainment channels. Long after the jump, the effect continues going strong, with viewers enjoying the rush toward the Earth over and over.

Of course, your brand does not need to plummet from space to earn a loyal audience. You simply need creative content offering something of value to your viewers. Done right, a brand can earn much more than a few views—it can earn a loyal following.

Owned media, on the other hand, offers the highest level of brand control. You control where and when the content is seen, how it is presented, and, quite often, even who is allowed to see it. Sometimes this means the viewers come directly to the brand's site, even *asking for permission* to read, watch, or participate.

The visitors to owned media sites are not merely interested, they are *actively seeking* the message you want to give them. For example, American Express has its OPEN forum, a content marketing hub for small businesses that is also considered its top lead for new card members. Operating successfully since 2007, OPEN forum engages its visitors in a three-tiered manner.

First, most of the content is there to drive brand awareness. The content for this purpose is meaningful to a wide audience, offering practical information geared toward small businesses that is highly shareable. Importantly, these selections not only avoid selling, they have little or nothing to do with the actual services offered by American Express. It is just free, useful information designed to appeal to the brand's target demographic, while also establishing OPEN forum as a go-to place for answers or information.

The second tier is about evaluation, not of the content, but of the consumer. Content of a more valuable or more specialized nature is made available—still free of charge—to those visitors interested in becoming members of the site. In exchange for membership, users offer certain demographic information about themselves which American Express may then utilize to filter leads for potential sales prospects.

The final tier of the OPEN forum's structure is realized through its Card Member Spotlight, a series of case studies demonstrating how using the American Express card and its related services have helped small businesses achieve their goals. By presenting these examples, which make up only a small portion of the offerings through OPEN Forum, American Express speaks directly to small business owners and managers already loyal to the brand through the use of the site and its plethora of owned media. Many of these site visitors will see these case studies and decide to become card members.

The best use of owned media is when the content is strong enough to draw visitors, yet valuable enough to keep them coming back. Whether the value comes from being a good reference, from entertainment value, or a combination of the two, the result is still a more direct relationship between the brand and its audience.

Getting Your Video Out There

Once you have a video representing your business and brand, the next step is figuring out how to get people to see it. There is a growing number of distribution channels available for your video content. And as the options increase, you will continue to see a wider array of pricing schemes.

While it's possible to spend quite a bit to place your video in front of potential viewers, some of the best results are often achieved without any additional hard costs. We frequently encounter brands who have failed to do something as simple as placing video content predominantly on an existing website. If the content shines and represents your brand, let it do the heavy lifting for you.

Consulting with an IT professional is always a smart decision at this stage; however, an experienced producing partner can also be of assistance in gauging your needs. Ultimately, some research into service providers will be necessary to ensure your site is able to serve your media to your audience in an optimal manner as you build a video library for your site that will keep viewers returning and help grow your brand.

While it may seem to be something out of the *Field of Dreams'* fantasy realm, the idea that *if you build it, they will come* has become something of a reality with online media. Using simple marketing tools like social media, viewers can discover your content at little or no cost to you.

Once your brand has established a following on services like Instagram, Twitter, Facebook or Tumblr, it is easy to virtually place your content right on the viewer's desktop, while also offering a link directly back to your own site to make the best use of your owned media space. By learning Search Engine Optimization (SEO) techniques and carefully placing keywords and links throughout your pages, you can also ensure major search engines favor your content for search results.

When you have a crucial understanding of your customers (who they are, where they are, and what they need), you can begin to anticipate what they will be doing or looking for and how to ensure their needs are met. Your website should also have a mechanism in place to track visits from social media sites, capturing demographics on your visitors, as well as allowing you to follow and respond to engagement on the various social media platforms. Knowledge equals power, and in this case, the more you know about your potential customers will empower your company to respond directly to their needs and wants, turning potential consumers into active customers.

By the way, even if your website does not have the storage space or streaming capabilities for presenting your video, you can still host a site offering a rich media experience. As discussed, YouTube has fabulous tools for creating a station of your own and making it simple to embed videos directly on your own webpages.

Because YouTube is integrated in the Google product offering, it tends to rank well in related searches. YouTube also offers ways to tag your videos for search robots in the same ways you can use SEO strategy via your written material. Another bonus of using a service like YouTube is that your videos, while offering potential links back to your site, may also function independently; a channel on YouTube can involve multiple related videos, independent of your company's site, offering your viewers and potential customers multiple ways to discover and navigate your messaging material.

Various Online Ad Types

Linear Ads

If you are interested in purchasing advertising time for your video content, it is essential to understand the different types of online video ads. Amongst the available options are linear video ads, also known as in-stream ads. These ads load into a video player onscreen either before, during, or just after another piece of video content plays, such as an entertainment program.

They appear in the main video player window where the content the viewer has chosen to watch will also play, in much the same way television commercials air along with the programs they support. The fees paid by advertisers in this manner increasingly support efforts of video producers to offer content "free" to the viewer, while still allowing them to monetize their product.

Linear video ads fall into the following categories:

Pre-roll ads

Pre-roll ads display prior to the main video content. Viewers must see these ads in order to watch the main feature, but the risk is viewers will give up and click away before the ad is finished.

Mid-roll ads

Mid-roll ads play at some point during the main video content. The upside is that viewers are already hooked into the content, making them less likely to click away. The potential downside is that interruption can be annoying enough to drive away some viewers.

Post-roll ads

Post-roll ads display after the main video content is complete. Obviously, these ads are the least intrusive, but there is also little to no incentive for the viewer to stick around long enough to watch them.

User ad-choice overlay

A user ad-choice overlay offers viewers a selection of ads from which to choose. After a default period of time, an ad will play automatically. Some viewers appreciate the chance to select the ad they view, but others may find the wait annoying and will click away.

Interactive video ads

Interactive video ads pause playback on the main content and invite the viewer to take action: to click for further information or to close the ad window.

Non-Linear Ads

It is also possible to purchase non-linear video ads, which function in a slightly different manner by not interfering with the flow of the main featured content. Many viewers prefer these types of ads because they do not require the experience to be interrupted or held up by the advertising.

Non-linear video ads fall into the following categories:

Overlay video

Overlay video ads run simultaneously with video content, usually as an interactive banner ad on top of the main video. Clicking on these ads generally pauses the content and takes the viewer to a full ad or to an advertiser's website. Some ads will collapse into a smaller "bug," while others have a "close" action that does the same thing.

Non-overlay video

Non-overlay video ads run concurrently with the video content in the media player but not on top of the main video content. These are similar to overlay ads but avoid the negative impact of covering the video content.

Companion ads

Companion ads display in a different window, alongside the main viewing content.

In-banner video

In-banner video ads play video in a standard banner size and placement that may or may not be expandable. These can be companion ads or stand-alone placements on pages without video players.

In-page video

In-page video ads are embedded video players specifically designed to show a video ad with no other attached video content.

In-text video

In-text video ads are user-initiated ads. When the user rolls over highlighted text on a web page, an overlay pops up and plays video associated with the highlighted word.

In-feed video

With the emergence of Snapchat and Instagram's stories, these platforms have to inject ads into your friend's stories in order for you to view them on their full mobile screen platform. Easily skippable, these ads need to grab the viewers' attention within the first three seconds; otherwise, an impression isn't guaranteed.

Sponsorship graphics

Sponsorship graphics frame the main video window and persist throughout the playing of its content.

In-game video

In-game video ads display during a game's loading or in between game levels.

Connected TV video ads

Connected TV video ads are associated with apps and can play in a variety of different ways.

Game console video ads

Game console video ads run on the dashboard of game consoles.

In-Story video ads

With Snapchat and Instagram's "Story" feature, brands can now inject their vertical videos into users' story feeds, prompting users to "swipe up" to reveal a new page.

Final Distribution Considerations

As you can see, there are quite a few methods for getting your video in front of viewers to leverage paid media as part of your branding strategy. Most of these options work best with short video segments; viewers may not be patient enough to wait through a longer clip unless the content is sufficiently engaging and valuable.

For this important reason, paid media tends to work best for quick sales pitches, brand introductions, and traditional advertising. It can be the lure that hooks a viewer and gets that click to happen, bringing a new potential customer to your owned media on your company website.

There are advertising platforms, like SpotX (spotxchange.com) processing over 5 billion ad decisions each day, delivering their content to over 600 million viewers in 190 countries. Do-it-yourself options also abound, like Google's TrueView campaigns, as well as Facebook's and Instagram's Business Tools.

These choices, as well as the requirements for how much of the content must be viewed or what constitutes a legitimate click, do change over time and according to each provider company's terms of use, so it is imperative any brand using an advertising service be familiar with current options. Additionally, there are also many sites (including private blogs and virtual magazines) that accept direct advertising. These are often outstanding options because you know your media will be seen by every visitor to that page and not left to the rules, restrictions, or whims of an ad placement service.

As we have discussed, earned media can be hosted virtually anywhere. If the content is valuable enough, it may not need its own website to thrive. Rather than trying to find its audience, the audience will seek out the media. The biggest decision required to get views started is to pick the service from which that video will stream.

Aside from YouTube, there are other viable services, like Vimeo and Veoh, allowing users to upload programming and make it available to a wide audience. Facebook is quickly gobbling up the market share when it comes to putting out video content. According to Social Media Today, the number is around 8 billion views a day. Also, younger companies, like Wistia, offer alternatives, including broader customization, as well as a different selection of analytics tools.

If your objectives for distribution are more for internal presentations or your existing customer base, partners, or targeted potential clients, there are also enterprise solutions available through a number of established providers. Using a service such as this will often allow for a greater ability to track users' actions, integrate with existing sign-in sites or subscriber services, and the avoidance of other third-party advertisements on the pages provided by user-generated content sites of the YouTube variety.

Providers such as Brightcove, Ustream, MediaCore and DaCast offer distinct services, ranging from live streaming to curated channels of pay-per-view content. In fact, the offerings of video hosting and delivery companies are evolving at a rapid rate, with new service options appearing with some frequency. For this reason, it is important to research all of the available choices amongst the dozens of international providers before making a final decision as to what will work best for your brand.

Choosing to use paid media or owned media will depend on a combination of your goals and the type of media itself. An established and knowledgeable production partner will also be able to help evaluate and guide these decisions, even before the media is produced. Having a complete plan in place prior to the creation of the media will assist in successful implementation of your marketing objectives.

Now that we have covered as many of the technical, practical, and theoretical aspects of content, production, and distribution as we can at this point, we are going to close the book with a chapter based on illustrative anecdotes from our own personal experiences, coupled with our predictions as to the future of video marketing.

CHAPTER THIRTEEN: Lessons Learned

"Don't waste a good mistake. Learn from it."

~Robert Kiyosaki, Investor

We've Made Mistakes, Too

Though we haven't had many truly bad video marketing experiences, we pride ourselves on not making the same mistake twice. There are many factors you can't always account for in the video world. Mishaps pop up all the time, but we try to find innovative ways to adapt to negative circumstances. Once an equipment box completely broke down, and we mean in pieces. Reacting quickly, as opposed to putting it off or waiting in despair, we bought a new one. Converting the former into a snowboard, we then pulled each other from the back of a minivan in a snowy Canadian parking lot, using the seatbelt as a tether and filming it for nothing more than our own personal enjoyment.

This is an example of something easy to handle, but we've had hairier moments, like the time a local gang kidnapped our director while filming in Jamaica. No, we are not making this up for dramatic effect, this happened in 2012. Before getting into the details, let's first state the root problem at the time was our inexperience managing multiple productions in multiple locations simultaneously.

In retrospect, we wish we had known how to properly plan better when first starting out. Instead, we simply did what we thought best and figured things out the hard way, suffering through painful lessons.

We would have meetings in which the decided course of action involved us interviewing our subjects, then figuring out what B-Roll to shoot thereafter, contingent upon the responses from our interviewee.

In theory, this makes sense, but if you were to look at our raw footage from the beginning stages of our company, you'd see 80 percent of the content is mediocre at best. The remaining 20 percent is what we used to create our signature work; so of course, in the end, it worked out, but the amount of wasted time our editors had to endure in the beginning is mind-boggling. Eventually, we scaled up to managing seven or eight different productions at the same time around the world, but if we knew back then what we know now, countless hours would have been saved.

Back to our Jamaican kidnapping story. The shoot was for a client possessing one of the biggest multi-national luxury hotel chains in the world. We were very excited since this was our first international hospitality campaign. However, we soon discovered that in developing countries things work quite differently. Operating in a place with less governmental organization and authority requires lateral thinking.

Our crew set up at Rick's Café, a tourist hangout overlooking the Caribbean Sea with steep, natural-formed cliffs, when our director came up with idea for the perfect shot. He wanted to capture a picturesque Steadicam glide running behind cliff-diving locals into the cove. In order to obtain the optimal vantage point, he needed to venture through a remote village to get to the other side, as the restaurant where our team was stationed and the desired location were separated by an unpassable inlet of cliffs and ocean.

When our director proposed the idea, our producer was all for it. "Just wave to us from the other side to get started," he told our director since the other cliff was so far away both teams had to shout to hear each other. At first, everything went fine. Though there was a group of 15 to 20 young men on our director's cliff, they didn't seem to pay him any attention. He started shooting tourists and locals cliff-diving as planned.

But then we noticed trouble brewing. The young men began closing in on our director, huddling around him. On the Rick's Cafe side, there was a guard armed with an AK-47 who proceeded to tell one of our crew members that a riot had recently erupted between these men, who were apparently in a gang, and the police. Ever since, they were banned from the café premises for soliciting drugs to tourists.

To the team's dismay, the gang drew in even tighter around our director, finally eclipsing their view of him. He was just gone.

One of the gang members dived off his side of the inlet, quickly scaling the 20-foot cliff where our team was perched. As he approached our crew he screamed, "Producer! Producer!" at the top of his lungs. He informed our team that his gang had just kidnapped our director. "He's our hostage," he said, "And if you wanna get him back, you need to pay up."

Our producer plastered a neutral face, although everyone's hearts were beating outside of their chests. They don't teach you how to handle situations like this at USC's business school. With only $80 collectively in their pockets, what would the gang do to our director if they couldn't pay up? Trying to stay calm, our producer asked the man how much the gang wanted.

The answer surprised our team. "Five hundred dollars," said the man.

This was a novel amount, considering our director had nearly $10,000 worth of equipment on him, but

there was something about the way the Jamaican presented the offer that triggered our producer's bullshit
meter. He now knew he wasn't dealing with sophisticated cartel members demanding a million-dollar payoff; these were local gang bangers looking for an easy
score to supplement their drug income.

He called the gangster's bluff. "That's ridiculous.
Get out of here."

The gangster, overtaken by our lack of perceived
empathy and fear, backed down a bit. After some back
and forth, he eventually agreed to $40 instead of $500.
Our producer balked again, knowing that he had the
advantage, so long as he remained coolheaded. Still,
the gangster was insistent. He told the team that if
they didn't pay up, we would never see our camera
equipment again, either.

Quickly devising a plan, our producer offered to
pay $20 upfront on the condition the gangster person-
ally agreed to walk our director back to Rick's Café.
Only then would he pay the other half. The gangster
took the $20, whistled to his buddies, and jumped off
the cliff to swim back to the other side.

As the minutes passed, the team waited nervously
for our director's return, hoping the gang would honor
their word. At last, a new gangster came trotting by,
squeezing our director by the arm. When he reached
our team, he demanded $100. It suddenly dawned on
our producer that the gangsters weren't even communicating with each other. They had no idea what deal
had been made for our director's release.

Emboldened by the gang's ignorance, one of our
crew members pulled our director back to the other
side of the security guy with the assault rifle. Then our

producer told the Jamaican in his calmest voice, "No, no, no. We already paid your friend everything."

Cowed, the gangster backed down and returned to his side, empty handed. After confirming our director was not only okay, but had gotten an amazing shot of the same gang members cliff-diving, the team quickly gathered their things.

Before getting in the cab, they heard shouting from the other cliff. After the second gangster returned to the others, a fight broke out between him and the first gangster as each accused the other of lying about the missing ransom money. By the time the gang regrouped and as our crew quick sped out of Negril, Jamaica in route to our client's five-star resort, our crew could hear them screaming, "Producer! You owe us money! Producer!"

The vital lesson we learned from this extreme encounter is to always keep your cool, especially when in danger. We got through what could have been a far worse situation by faking a calm demeanor to wrest control of the situation.

This experience also cemented our resolve to learn as much as possible about the surroundings and customs of foreign locations prior to any future shoot. For instance, if we had known going into Jamaica how hostilities had recently flared due to a drug crackdown and how problems might spill over to visiting Americans, the team would have proceeded far differently.

Technical Blunders

Let's change gears now and talk about other mistakes that led to important lessons. This next one wasn't as dangerous, but it was certainly instructive.

It occurred in Kansas City when we were working on a live satellite broadcast between two locations for a corporate client.

A live stream bridged the video link so both groups could communicate in real time. Because we booked the job just two days before, we had to use a team unfamiliar with the equipment and the area of Kansas City. Not only that, there were technical issues. The satellite connection wasn't great. It also happened to be our first time working with this client, and since it was only an hour-long broadcast, we couldn't just stop to fix an issue and restart. The show had to go on, even though we had major audio problems.

The audio was bad. *Really bad.* It sounded like a dog barking on the live broadcast every time the mic popped. We were also picking up static and microphone noise, so for anyone watching online it sounded like there were dogs loose and people chatting in the background. In addition, you could barely hear what the speaker was saying.

Needless to say, this was not the ideal way for a video production company to begin a relationship with an important new client. The online comments we received didn't help our image, either. Someone wrote: "Can anyone shut that dog up?" Another asked why there were so many people talking in the background. "I feel like I'm in a movie theater."

Such negativity was hard to swallow. Fortunately, we had signed a three-broadcast contract; otherwise, this client would probably never have worked with us again. We reacted quickly, redeeming ourselves on the next production by using a much better team and equipment to produce a seamless broadcast and satellite uplink. From this experience, we learned to accept blame early on, remedy our mistakes as soon as possible, revise our approach, and relaunch.

It Pays to Be Flexible in Mind and Approach

There have been times when we dreamed up an idea, thinking it would be the next viral video, but, instead, it fell flat. By the way, if this happens to you, it doesn't necessarily mean your content is bad. It could mean your distribution strategy isn't right. You may not be reaching the right target audience or obtaining the desired media impressions. This happens to us occasionally with corporate clients who don't reserve enough funds to do a media buy to start video seeding. Consequently, the video doesn't reach influential individuals.

This is a valid concern, but it's also brought home the realization that creativity, humor, and overall quality is always in the eye of the beholder. We may think something is great, yet it doesn't resonate with our target audience.

Testing with focus groups, even if it means simply calling five to ten people or conducting a random survey online, has been beneficial. We often use this approach to try out ideas to see if a concept is working. Though we may think something is a winner, others might not feel the same. It's been crucial for us to adapt to any market feedback.

Flexibility is also necessary, though we typically aren't unprepared for a video shoot and, as previously mentioned, we pride ourselves on being the Navy Seals of video production. What this means is we can be anywhere in the world within 48 hours. Because we have good people, we can adapt to a changing environment.

For instance, unforeseen problems arise. Sometimes locations are not ready yet or are unavailable, forcing us to figure out contingency plans. We've worked on projects in which we only got the call one week prior. One such time, we had to arrange a full-scale, six-figure production for a client. Ultimately, we knocked it out of the park because we had the right people in the right place and fortunately got lucky with the weather and location. However, the truth is, in the production world, you can create your own luck if you plan well and use capable, quality people.

Other Companies are Doing It Wrong. We Learned from Their Mistakes

Many organizations are caught up in antiquated ways of thinking. When it comes to marketing, they are un-original, recreating the same content again and again, hoping to achieve different results.

The shampoo industry is a prime example. We've all seen the commercial of the celebrity throwing their hair around. It's shimmering, and they're smiling as they say, "I'm a Revlon girl or guy." The problem is, it's nearly always the same ad, reskinned with a new product or copy. Rarely does a company break this stifling mold. Even if they do change it up for a time, they typically revert to what "works."

The real reason for lack of creativity within the marketing world hinges on a hierarchy in continuous disruption. The average CMO has a job for two-and-a-half years or less. The typical agency personnel will stay in a position for approximately 18 months before either jumping to another company or moving to a different account. We've heard from clients who were initially wowed by the pitch from the agency's creative director, only to find out their budget earned them the B Team.

There is this influx, not only on the agency side, but in the brand world. The people involved don't want to get fired; they don't want change. Consequently, they try to hold onto what they can by recreating the same content, hoping for different results. This phenomenon is pronounced in many bigger brands and as mentioned prior, 95 percent of Fortune 500 companies have lost market share due to this exact reason.

From a marketing standpoint, there aren't many companies attempting real innovation, trying things fundamentally different, thought-provoking, and creative while still managing to be on-brand. After working with some of these groups, we've seen firsthand the political nature of, *"Well, I can't do that because that's not part of our brand essence,"* or some other disingenuous answer. The emergence and inevitable success of countless Kickstarter and Indiegogo companies is case in point for how an innovative product, story, or video can engage an audience 10 times better then repurposing stale content.

The reality is they don't want to push the envelope and start breaking things because it threatens their job security. Individuals don't want to upset their boss. They don't want to get the CEO's attention in a negative light because it's risky. If you stick your neck out for a fundamentally different idea, you risk your job because if it doesn't work, someone has to take the blame. Corporate will need to point a finger, and you may face the consequences as the imbecile who took the risk and came up with the bad idea.

Now and then, however, a person or brand tries something bold and different, the risk paying off in full. A good example is Frito Lay and the Doritos "Crash the Super Bowl" campaign. The idea was for consumers to submit commercials online. The grand prize winner would go on to win a million dollars and be featured in the Super Bowl.

This campaign has been going on since 2006, so it's easy to forget that when this concept was originated, it was groundbreaking. No one wanted to do it at Frito Lay. Rudy Wilson, the VP of Marketing at Pepsico at the time, had to fight for this vision to be implemented because everyone had doubts. *What if no one submitted anything? What if the submissions were so horrible they couldn't even be shown on TV?*

Wilson, along with the rest of his marketing team at Goodby, Silverstein & Partners had to face these concerns and questions. He and the others risked their jobs coming up with an original idea. Before that, every chip commercial was predictable. It typically featured some funny dialogue or a somewhat interesting storyline, but the ads were anything but unique.

Now, because of Wilson and his team, Doritos suddenly had thousands of submissions from customers going over and beyond to create an awesome commercial. The upshot was a win-win for the creators and Doritos. Not only might some lucky winner receive major media time as the Super Bowl commercial winner, but Doritos had the opportunity to broadcast the second, third, and fourth place contestants, creating even more buzz for their brand.

Any lingering concern over submission quality was soon mitigated; the received commercials were so good it absolutely made sense to feature them. In hindsight, just think how well this risk turned out for Doritos. Frito Lay is no stranger to seven-figure production budgets for broadcast commercials, but now due to some brave new thinking, they have a whole series of crowd-sourced content created by fans, promoted by more fans, and voted on for quality.

The submissions were picked based on the number of social shares and likes, of course, ensuring huge mass market appeal. In addition, they received even more free distribution by publicly listing the commercial winner during the Super Bowl, capitalizing on the great story that brought this all about. Again, in retrospect, it's easy to dismiss this example and other once novel ideas that appear excellent in hindsight. Too often, we forget they were originally thought of as crazy or asinine. It took forward-thinking individuals willing to risk their stature and employment to bring them to fruition, but that's what it takes to create something remarkable within a conservative, fear-based industry.

How to Prepare for Video Production's Future Now

Video production is going to change because the mediums will change. As we've already seen throughout social media and with mobile media's exponential growth, vertically framed video is taking off. In case you've been living in a cave for the past 5 years, vertical video is 9 x 16 formatted video, as opposed to the traditional wide screen 16 x 9 horizontal frame that you'll see on TV. It works because the platforms where users are viewing the content is natively vertical. It's disruptive to turn your phone on its side in a platform when you're used to a singular setting to absorb content.

A TV, however, sits on its side, so the image seen is long on top and short on the sides. This works because your eyes prefer to see this horizontally. Putting horizontal videos on vertical platforms, and vice versa, is suboptimal. It's better to shoot video so it matches the display your most valuable audience members will experience it on. When shooting vertically, you have a much shorter frame length; and thus the subject needs to be front and center, reducing what can be seen around the sides and behind the subject.

An interesting contrast is Instagram's news feed, which is mostly horizontal or square. Facebook is also mostly horizontal. Both are slowly integrating vertical video into their platforms, as well as augmented reality (AR) and virtual reality (VR) formats. The key for these platforms is understanding how mobile audiences are viewing any content you produce. Square video on Instagram and Facebook mobile has performed up to 20 percent better than widescreen alone in the past for some of our brands. Reason being, as a user scrolls through content, the square video takes up more surface area or pixels on the user's phone; consequently, they're more likely to see and engage with the content as it's on their screen for a longer period of time.

In response to changing media trends, brands are now integrating vertical video into their marketing strategies because that's how users are viewing content. Snapchat, for instance, built their platform on vertical video as that's how users naturally will film content on their smartphone.

As far as video production's future, we know media platforms will evolve. As they do, so will the way users consume content. What won't change is storytelling's importance. Being able to connect with someone and have them think differently and cognitively about your brand will stay the same.

Even so, there will be new ways to connect with consumers, whether it be 360-degree video or virtual reality content. The latter, as well as augmented reality, are two things trending very much as 3-D video did back in 2009-2010. What's so interesting about 360-degree video is its ability to capture everything around you, literally everything. The camera technology itself is formidable at current; however, the quality and process are becoming easier to manage.

As of 2017, one of the great devices is a Gear 360 Camera by Samsung.

This technology is amazing because it allows an audience to frame the story. You, the creator, don't necessarily have control of where their eye goes. You can add details to make the focus what you prefer, but for the most part, it's an immersive, *user-generated* experience. If done well, it can create something so powerful users obtain a visceral sense of living in an entirely different space.

Now, of course, the technology isn't as real as we want it to be yet, but there are good products providing unprecedented deep immersion. For instance, you can put on a headset and be entirely whisked away to a $50-million Patagonian mansion for a real estate tour.

Doubtless, virtual reality will continue to grow in use and ubiquity, especially since Samsung is giving away Gear Headsets with every Samsung Galaxy phone purchase. In the future, there will be millions of unbelievable new devices in the public's hands, spurring fantastic new technological usage. Will these new cameras and technology be something people use every single day? Probably not. However, their emerging presence is yet another unique way for brands to connect, create a lasting impression with consumers.

Theoretical Implications of Our Video Future

Let's get philosophical for a second. Ask yourself this: when there are no more Internet bandwidth restrictions, when you can communicate, watch, and do anything on the web for free, what does that world look like? When you don't have to worry about data limitations and you're able to do things like stream video content anywhere in the world, what else is going to happen? What other inventions or technology will emerge when everything is Google Fiber speed?

We predict video will be even more prominent than it is today. We are witnessing a trend in which "hyper-content" is becoming increasingly more enjoyable and viral than straight interviews or traditional video fare. Few people want to sit down and watch a 10-minute interview, even if it pertains to a subject matter they really like. However, they will watch a 30-second clip on how to create a great chicken piccata from start to finish. As technology increases, as we get faster at being able to maneuver with everything being instantaneous, video content will need to do the same, whether it be sped up interviews, cliff notes of interviews, or employing a virtual office remotely.

Many of these trends are clearly already happening, but in the future important questions will be: *How do you condense video further? How do you make it go faster? How do you enable it so someone can absorb your content even quicker than having to watch a full interview?*

How to Not Get Left Behind: The Packed Bar Strategy

Many video tactics employed just a few years back are now irrelevant. Let's consider why and how you can learn from what no longer works. There are hundreds of social media platforms no one has ever heard of. They perished because the market didn't react to them. Users didn't jump onboard, or they couldn't earn enough advertising revenue and they disappeared.

Vine is a textbook example in which users decided they didn't like the platform anymore. There are valuations and KPI's to determine the performance of an organization based on items such as net revenue or customer loyalty. As in the case of Vine, when a channel doesn't have the proper user base and isn't hitting certain advertising impressions to stay afloat, it dies.

Let's consider a success story now. Facebook dominates today because they took a strategic approach to how they launched, exclusively opening their platform with college students to gain momentum in the beginning. *It was cool.* All of your friends were on it. You could use it to find out if the hot guy down the hall had a girlfriend. Of course, there's much more to Facebook's success than this. They also found a unique way to get people's attention, encouraging them to join their platform. Once people were on it, that's when the critical mass really kicked in. Then everyone wanted to get in on it.

You can think about critical mass like a good party. No one wants to party alone. Even if some gathering has the sickest drinks and the best band, no one wants to go if it's dead inside. On the flip side, if the party's packed to the brim—even if they are serving cheap booze behind the bar—it doesn't matter. *People want to be in that bar.* That's the key to social media.

Beyond that, ease of use matters. Facebook's algorithms create a news feed where content most relevant to you is on top. Applying the Kaizen approach, Facebook keeps seeking to improve, giving its users a better experience. Their goal is to keep you on their platform for as long as possible. The longer you scroll through posts, the more advertisements you see and the more revenue they make. With that said, it's in their best interest to create a platform where you can custom tailor your feed to display exactly what you want. It's little wonder people keep returning.

Going back to Vine, it's obvious they recognized the packed bar strategy; only their users took the free drinks and went to another club. The Vine strategists' mistaken thinking probably went something like this, "Okay. We're going to get all of these individuals to make Vines for us, and it's going to be really short content because that's what people prefer." The problem is YouTube benefited more from Vine than the other way around because it was difficult to find quality Vines. Thousands of "Vine Highlight Videos" surfaced on YouTube in the wake of Vine's launch. In this situation, there was too much noise and content on the platform itself, and the user experience made it difficult to find the good stuff.

Understanding *where* the audience is, understanding *how* they're reacting to social media, and *why* they're actually observing the content is more important than a myopic strategy that stubbornly expects people to behave in a certain way without the right incentives.

Consider Snapchat in this context. There are interesting things about this channel, but there is also a huge problem. My opinion is that user fatigue will hit a maximum threshold at some point in the near future. Snapchat's uniqueness, with its disappearing messages and content that only lasts 24 hours can only take it so far without some serious innovation. We're already seeing Instagram dominate the story battle with Snapchat's daily active users dropping by 30 percent following the launch of Instagram's Stories in 2016. If Snapchat happened to be your only distribution method, how might you feel about your traffic dropping 30 percent overnight?

At some point, users will grow bored with it, and the second Snapchat stops innovating, it will die. Of course, that doesn't mean brands can't take advantage of it now—nor does it mean Snapchat will disappear like Vine. It possesses die-hard fans who love the platform, even if the probability that it will scale like Facebook is extremely slim. It's just something to constantly monitor. We have found it is good to always be wondering this: *where is my audience? How are they integrating/reacting to posted content, and ultimately, is this activity increasing my ROI?*

Predictions: Where Video Will Go from Here

It's fun and useful to contemplate what video marketing production will look like 5, 10, and 50 years from now. Within 5 years, as streaming content becomes even easier to access, not only from a 4K and higher resolution standpoint, but also wide-streaming 360-degree video, being able to bridge cameras together will facilitate a highly immersive experience.

This will be paramount for experiencing live events. Music festivals, concerts, and conferences are growing in popularity due to the full immersion experience eagerly sought by millennials. It's easy to see why. They want to be there but can't always be for a number of factors: time, logistics, and, of course, money. Especially as this generation starts buying houses, they won't have the disposable income to be there in person. So, what's the best alternative?

Virtual reality, of course. Having a VR headset or something equivalent that is so immersive it feels like you're there. Right now, there are significant limitations with this technology. With one camera, you're stuck with only a meager semblance of the actual experience. But what happens when affordable technology exists, allowing you to jump from one angle to another?

What will it feel like when you can literally move around wherever you want because there are so many cameras on the scene? Suddenly, you can view the band from the front row. Then the rafters. Then the mosh pit. You can even go backstage. The beauty of this technology is its uncanny ability to "transport" you, allowing you to seemingly be in all these different places at once on demand. This kind of technical capacity is perhaps only five years away. I'd like to think that ten years from now, VR will be so incredible people will be addicted to it. The negative effects will be hugely impactful as actual reality will not be as rewarding as the world you can experience through your avatar.

Even if this dystopian future doesn't play out quite like the OASIS in Stephen Spielberg's film *Ready Play One,* it's important to think about VR's future this way. The merging of our physical reality with the virtual reality of the Sims videogame containing quality so real it's indistinguishable from the everyday world is a terrifying prospect, yet exciting. Fifty years from now, the possibilities are endless and too difficult to pin down. We may be living on Mars. On the other hand, fifty years from now, video as we know it will probably be boring. It won't be employed the way it is now. Perhaps it will only be used in an educational or nostalgic, archival-type reference purpose.

Breathtaking technological breakthroughs and unprecedented offshoots we can't even fathom now will fill this space. Augmented and virtual reality have the potential to provide an experience so immersive, engaging, exciting, and effective people won't bother with old-school video. They will also avoid doing much of the analogue activities we currently enjoy because the spectacle and thrill of futuristic new media will be so fun and entertaining.

Regardless of the path you choose from this point forward, whether it be creating your own in-house video production team or working with a team of experienced professionals, know that the medium or method users view content is going to change. It's how you adapt to this change that can fundamentally change your organization's path for years to come. You can't motivate audiences without a story, and your story can't change people's behavior unless it's true to your core, your why. Happy shooting.

GLOSSARY

Annotations:

Video Annotations are an uploader-controlled, dynamic overlay on videos that allows you to overlay text on a video and/or make parts of the video clickable. You can add, edit, and delete annotations to your videos, controlling the text, placement, timing, and link URLs.

Audience Retention:

The Audience Retention report (formerly known as Hot Spots Insight) measures your video's ability to retain its audience. It shows when viewers fast forward, rewind, or leave your video.

Avatar:

The square image on your channel page that represents your channel across the site.

Bulletin:

A message that channel owners can send to their subscribers. Bulletins show up in subscribers' feeds. Channel owners can attach videos to a bulletin.

Calls to Action (CTAs):

These prompt the viewer to take an action.

Channel or Channel Page:

YouTube.com/CHANNELNAME. A channel is the public page for a user account on YouTube. It contains uploaded videos, playlists, liked videos, favorited videos, channel comments, and general activity. Some creators manage or create content across multiple channels.

Comments:

These are written comments on videos, channels, playlists, or in response to other comments. Comments may be posted either on the watch page or on a channel page.

Community:

Any actions taken by a viewer on or around your channel and content. Includes likes, favorites, subscriptions, and comments.

Content Marketing:

The dissemination of valuable and consistent information to attract customers and build brands without selling.

Earned Media:

Media exposure or recognition you've earned through word-of-mouth (usually based on good content or distribution).

End-Card or End-Slate:

A graphic that creators include at the end of their videos. End-cards typically include specific Calls to Action to subscribe for more content or visit a channel page. They may also contain credits for the video. Generally, end-cards prominently feature annotations.

Engagement:

Interaction between the creator and the audience, the viewer and the video, or the creator and the site.

Can be measured by the number of interactions (comments, favorites, likes, or new subscriptions) per view.

Evergreen Content:

Content you can use indefinitely since it does not expire in the short term.

Favorite(s):

A user action that adds a video to their channel's Favorites playlist. This action can also be broadcast to subscribers.

Feed:

A stream of activity either for one channel (via the channel page feed) or for multiple channels (the homepage feed). Feed activities include uploads, updated playlists, video comments, channel comments, new subscriptions, bulletins, likes, favorites, and sharing. Users control what feed activities they broadcast and by subscribing to channels, what feed activities are broadcasted to them in their homepage feed.

Hangouts on Air:

Google+ Hangouts are a live video chatting feature, and they can be broadcast on your YouTube channel.

Hero Content:

Often requiring a bigger production budget and slicker production quality, hero content is meant to appeal to a mass audience.

Hook:

Content that is meant to keep viewers interested in what happens next. Ideally, a video's hook happens within the first 15 seconds.

Hosted Playlist:

A collection of videos linked by additional hosted videos. Hosted videos can act as intros, outros, and/or interstitials. Hosted videos can contain an actual host (person) or creative branding that acts as a host.

Hub Content:

Think: teasers or announcements. These videos are meant to keep an audience returning to your channel on a regular basis.

Hygiene Content:

Evergreen content with long-lasting permanence.

In-house Team:

A group of people fully capable of producing, shooting, and editing video content, particularly digital, but also broadcast media.

Interruptive Marketing:

The (often times annoying) promotional strategy of attention diversion.

Key Performance Indicator (KPI):

A measurable value demonstrating how effectively you are achieving business objectives to determine success.

Like(s):

A user action that shows appreciation for a video. This action can be broadcast to subscribers in the feed.

Metadata:

The textual information that describes a video, channel, or playlist. Video metadata includes title, tags, and description. Playlist metadata includes title and description. Channel metadata includes a description.

Optimization:

An action that increases the potential success of a video, channel, playlist, or content strategy.

Other Channels Module:

An optional module allowing the channel owner to feature other channels on their channel page.

Outsource Team:

An outside production company or organization of some kind primarily focused on creating content.

Owned Media:

The content you control, such as your company site, blog, and/or your social media channels.

Packaging

Graphics and/or content that adds context to a video. Packaging can build your brand, connect your host with the audience, add relevant context to archived content, or add scripted/annotated Calls to Action.

Paid Media:

An advertising channel a brand pays for. It may include things like display ads, television spots, sponsorships, paid search results, and Internet display ads.

Playlist:

A playlist is a collection of videos that can be viewed, shared, and embedded like an individual video. You can create playlists using any videos on YouTube.

Videos can be in multiple playlists. Uploaded videos and favorited videos are default playlists on your channel.

Pre-buzz:

Audience interest in a tent-pole event occurring in the days and weeks leading up to it.

Preditor:

One person responsible for fulfilling all of the video production tasks.

Programming:

The practice and strategy of organizing videos, shows, or channel content and activity into a daily, weekly, or season-long schedule.

Share:

Ability to distribute videos via social media, email, or direct links. This action can be broadcast to subscribers.

Suggested Videos:

Video thumbnails appearing in the right-hand column of watch pages and the homepage or the tiled thumbnails appearing when a video has finished playing.

Subscriber/Subscription:

By subscribing to a channel, users will see that channel's activity in their homepage feed. Subscribers can also opt into email communication from subscribed channels on a per-upload and weekly digest basis.

Subscriber Box:

See Other Channels Module.

Tags:

Words or phrases used to describe the content of your videos added to videos at time of upload (see Metadata).

Teaser:

A short video acting as a preview or trailer for longer content. Can be used to promote larger content initiatives or announcements.

Recommendation Activity:

A strategy in which a channel likes, favorites, or comments on a video in order to promote that video to their subscribers through the feed.

Series Playlist:

A playlist that locks the videos into one specific playlist. Meant for serial or episodic content following a narrative story arc in order to promote that video to their subscribers' playlists on the channel.

Templates:

Different pre-set channel designs that can be used to highlight videos, playlists, and other channels.

Tent-pole Programming and Publishing:

Content creation and publishing strategy meant to draft off of the popularity of large cultural events. Programming and publishing tent-pole content is meant to maximize audience.

Thumbnails:

The images selected to represent your videos or playlists on the site.

Traffic Source:

The referral source of a video view; the page, module, or site that drove a viewer to a video.

Vlog:

A video-blog. A casual, conversational video format or genre featuring a person talking directly to camera.

Watch Page:

The page where the majority of video viewing happens. URLs with the format youtube.com/watch?v=[video ID Here] are watch pages.

Watch Time:

The amount of time in aggregate that your viewers are watching your videos. Watch time is estimated in Analytics.

YouTube Analytics:

A tool providing information across various metrics for videos, channels, and audience. Available in your user account.

33634949R00131

Made in the USA
San Bernardino, CA
24 April 2019